Body Farms

Other titles in the Crime Scene Investigations series:

Body Farms

by Diane Yancey

LUCENT BOOKS
A part of Gale, Cengage Learning

GALE
CENGAGE Learning™

Detroit • New York • San Francisco • New Haven, Conn • Waterville, Maine • London

© 2009 Gale, Cengage Learning

LIBRARY OF CONGRESS CATALOGING-IN-PUBLICATION DATA

Yancey, Diane.
   Body farms / by Diane Yancey.
      p. cm. -- (Crime scene investigations)
   Includes bibliographical references and index.
   ISBN 978-1-4205-0106-3 (hardcover)
1. Human decomposition--Research--Tennessee--Juvenile literature. 2. Human
skeleton--Analysis--Juvenile literature. 3. Forensic osteology--Tennessee--Juvenile
literature. 4. Crime laboratories--Tennessee--Juvenile literature. 5. Bass, William M.,
1928--Juvenile literature. 6. Forensic anthropology--United States--Juvenile literature.
I. Title.
   QP87.Y36 2009
   599.9--dc22
                                                                      2008053697

Lucent Books
27500 Drake Rd
Farmington Hills MI 48331

ISBN-13: 978-1-4205-0106-3
ISBN-10: 1-4205-0106-2

Printed in the United States of America
1 2 3 4 5 6 7 13 12 11 10 09

Contents

Foreword

The popularity of crime scene and investigative crime shows on television has come as a surprise to many who work in the field. The main surprise is the concept that crime scene analysts are the true crime solvers, when in truth, it takes dozens of people, doing many different jobs, to solve a crime. Often, the crime scene analyst's contribution is a small one. One Minnesota forensic scientist says that the public "has gotten the wrong idea. Because I work in a lab similar to the ones on *CSI*, people seem to think I'm solving crimes left and right—just me and my microscope. They don't believe me when I tell them that it's just the investigators that are solving crimes, not me."

Crime scene analysts do have an important role to play, however. Science has rapidly added a whole new dimension to gathering and assessing evidence. Modern crime labs can match a hair of a murder suspect to one found on a murder victim, for example, or recover a latent fingerprint from a threatening letter, or use a powerful microscope to match tool marks made during the wiring of an explosive device to a tool in a suspect's possession.

Probably the most exciting of the forensic scientist's tools is DNA analysis. DNA can be found in just one drop of blood, a dribble of saliva on a toothbrush, or even the residue from a fingerprint. Some DNA analysis techniques enable scientists to tell with certainty, for example, whether a drop of blood on a suspect's shirt is that of a murder victim.

While these exciting techniques are now an essential part of many investigations, they cannot solve crimes alone. "DNA doesn't come with a name and address on it," says the Minnesota forensic scientist. "It's great if you have someone in custody to match the sample to, but otherwise, it doesn't help.

That's the investigator's job. We can have all the great DNA evidence in the world, and without a suspect, it will just sit on a shelf. We've all seen cases with very little forensic evidence get solved by the resourcefulness of a detective."

While forensic specialists get the most media attention today, the work of detectives still forms the core of most criminal investigations. Their job, in many ways, has changed little over the years. Most cases are still solved through the persistence and determination of a criminal detective whose work may be anything but glamorous. Many cases require routine, even mind-numbing tasks. After the July 2005 bombings in London, for example, police officers sat in front of video players watching thousands of hours of closed-circuit television tape from security cameras throughout the city, and as a result were able to get the first images of the bombers.

The Lucent Books Crime Scene Investigations series explores the variety of ways crimes are solved. Titles cover particular crimes such as murder, specific cases such as the killing of three civil rights workers in Mississippi, or the role specialists such as medical examiners play in solving crimes. Each title in the series demonstrates the ways a crime may be solved, from the various applications of forensic science and technology to the reasoning of investigators. Sidebars examine both the limits and possibilities of the new technologies and present crime statistics, career information, and step-by-step explanations of scientific and legal processes.

The Crime Scene Investigations series strives to be both informative and realistic about how members of law enforcement—criminal investigators, forensic scientists, and others—solve crimes, for it is essential that student researchers understand that crime solving is rarely quick or easy. Many factors—from a detective's dogged pursuit of one tenuous lead to a suspect's careless mistakes to sheer luck to complex calculations computed in the lab—are all part of crime solving today.

"Ghastly Affront to Human Dignity"

On a sunny, spring day in 1985, a survey crew began laying out boundaries for a new parking lot behind the University of Tennessee Medical Center in Knoxville, Tennessee. The expansion was going to include parts of a former dump site: a sloping patch of ground covered with trees, brush, and honeysuckle vines. The crew worked hard all morning and at noon took their lunches and found patches of shade where they could rest and eat. One young man chose a particularly inviting spot and began munching on a sandwich, flapping away a few flies that seemed determined to share his food.

He soon discovered that flies were not the only unpleasant occupants of the site. As his eyes roved over the undergrowth, he noticed what appeared to be a human shape half hidden by bushes and surrounded by a chain-link fence. Horrified, he looked closer. There was no mistake—a corpse lay on a cement slab in the center of a clearing. And even more horrifying, there were several more human bodies lying beside it. To his disgust, he realized that the flies that pestered him had been going back and forth between the corpses as well.

The man hurried to report his shocking discovery to his fellow workers. They informed him that he had stumbled upon a research project being carried out by an anthropology professor at the university. The professor, William M. Bass, was studying human decomposition by allowing corpses to decay in the open air. There had already been an article about the university's Anthropology Research Facility in the local Knoxville newspaper, and outraged readers had written editorials that protested what they called a "ghastly affront [insult] to human dignity."[1]

University of Tennessee anthropology professor and forensics expert William Bass. Bass's studies include human body decomposition on so-called body farms.

Protests and Privacy

When the young man from the survey crew went home that night, he told his mother about his unpleasant experience. She, too, was shocked and, being a member of a local advocacy group called Solutions to Issues of Concern to Knoxvillians (SICK), decided to take action. Within days, members of SICK rallied to voice disapproval of Bass's work, holding a demonstration outside the facility and carrying signs that read, "This Makes Us S.I.C.K."[2] The group was especially indignant that such experiments were being carried out in plain view of the general population.

Bass met with the protesters and explained that the facility was not designed to shock or offend, but to carry out

Practical Science

Forensic anthropology is the application of anthropological research and techniques to help establish important facts about decomposing remains and human skeletons. The science is practical and involves the following subfields:

- forensic osteology: The study of the skeleton.
- forensic archaeology: The collection and removal of human remains from a scene.
- forensic taphonomy: The study of environmental conditions, trauma, and decomposition that affect human remains after death.

groundbreaking work that would help law enforcement solve murders. The bodies were closely watched over, treated with respect, and the bones carefully stored when the experiments were complete. The crisis passed, but the professor realized that the chain-link fence around the small cement slab was an inadequate barrier. The entire 2.5-acre (1ha) facility needed to be screened from the public's eyes.

He therefore turned to university chancellor Jack Reese, who quickly provided funds for a chain-link fence around the entire perimeter of the research area. Shortly thereafter, an 8-foot-high (2.4m) wooden privacy fence was also erected inside the chain-link enclosure, discouraging curiosity seekers and protecting unwitting passersby from disturbing sights.

New Respect

With the protest over, research continued unchecked and virtually unnoticed behind the fences of Bass's facility until 1993. Then, bestselling novelist Patricia Cornwell came for a visit and went on to write about a "decay research facility" in her fifth novel, a thriller titled *The Body Farm*. The book drew attention to Bass's outdoor lab and gave it the enduring nickname, "the Body Farm." "Patricia says she didn't coin that term," Bass says. "[She] went to a lecture at the FBI Academy, and one of [the agents], Irving Futrell comes in and says, 'I've just gotten back from the Body Farm.' And she wrote that down for her book. So, I think it was coined by an FBI agent and used in a meeting at the FBI Academy and picked up by Patricia Cornwell."[3]

In the years that followed, the Body Farm gained the respect of the scientific community as a site of some of the most important developments ever to be made in forensic science.

An "Aha" Moment

William M. Bass had no intention of becoming a forensic anthropologist until a chance incident in 1955 changed his life forever. He describes the moment during an interview with HarperCollins publishers:

I was in graduate school at the University of Kentucky . . . working on a master's degree in counseling. Just for fun, I was also taking a course in anthropology, and one day my anthropology professor, Dr. Charlie Snow, asked if I wanted to go with him on an identification case. Dr. Snow was a well known "bone detective," as forensic anthropologists were called back then, and he'd been asked to identify the burned body of a woman who was killed in a fiery head-on collision. While we were out there in the field that day, I had one of those life-changing "aha" moments, and the next week, I switched from counseling to anthropology. Besides changing the course of my life, that's the only case that's ever made me throw up!

Quoted in HarperCollins, "Author Interview: Dr. Bill Bass on *Beyond the Body Farm*," HarperCollins, www.harpercollins.com/author/authorExtra.aspx?authorID=32695&isbn13 =9780060875299&displayType=bookinterview.

Bass retired in 1999, and one of his former students, anthropologist Richard Jantz, became director of what has developed into the Forensic Anthropology Center. The center includes the Body Farm, skeletal collections, and a computer data bank of skeletal measurements and other information.

Jantz is just as passionate about the work at the center as Bass was. Through both men's efforts, studies done there continue to provide new insights into human death and decomposition. Forensic experts, law enforcement officials, and the public have become more accepting of human decomposition research, and other body farms have been established. The second, the Forensic Osteology Research Station (FOREST), opened in 2006 in conjunction with Western Carolina University in the Blue Ridge Mountains of North Carolina. The Forensic Anthropology Facility at Texas State, located on Texas State University's Freeman Ranch near the small town of San Marcos, opened in 2008. Sam Houston State University in Huntsville, Texas, began construction of its own body farm—the Southeast Texas Applied Forensic Science Facility—in 2008 as well.

Thirst for Knowledge

Because the body farms are in different parts of the country, each has a slightly different focus. In Tennessee, researchers pursue a broad range of study into decomposition under all conditions. In Western Carolina, they emphasize decomposition in the mountainous region of the Carolinas. In Texas, they focus on decomposition issues in desert locales. One issue, for example, is the presence of vultures. Being able to recognize beak marks, scratch marks, and dung deposits on a decayed corpse is vital in Texas. Texas State anthropology professor Michelle Hamilton says, "This is the kind of information we need to get in the hands of law enforcement and other anthropologists, to say things are different in different areas."[4]

Researchers at body farms continually look for new and better ways to determine the postmortem interval (PMI)—the time between death and the discovery of a body. They also work to find new ways to identify badly decomposed remains and to locate bodies hidden by forensically savvy murderers. With enthusiasm and determination, they believe that no project is too outlandish and no exertion too great if it produces valid information. Their thirst for knowledge causes them to view errors and setbacks as fresh incentives to new efforts.

Bass's own story is a perfect example of their point of view. After a humiliating mistake that made him a laughingstock and haunted him for decades, the professor took the episode and made it a jumping-off point for a new life project. "Personally, I was embarrassed; scientifically, I was intrigued; above all, I was determined to do something about it,"[5] he recalls in his book *Death's Acre*, which he wrote with journalist and documentary filmmaker Jon Jefferson. How Bass's mistake triggered unparalleled advances in criminal investigation is not only a fascinating tale, but it is also the story of the founding of the first body farm.

CHAPTER 1

An Embarrassing Mistake

Forensic anthropologist William M. Bass became convinced of the need to study human decomposition in 1978, as the result of a miscalculation that he would never live down. It was December 29, 1977, when he got a telephone call from a Tennessee county Sheriff's Department, asking him to investigate an apparent murder in the small town of Franklin. Bass was Tennessee's state forensic anthropologist, a consultant with the Tennessee Bureau of Investigation, and head of the Anthropology Department at the University of Tennessee at Knoxville. A forensic anthropologist is a specialist who uses the human skeleton to answer questions of identity and trauma in medical and criminal cases. Because of his position and expertise, Bass was the person that law enforcement called when a badly decayed corpse needed to be examined.

The Headless Corpse

Upon arrival in Franklin, Bass learned that the body in question had been found in a private family cemetery on the grounds of a historic Tennessee estate. The estate was owned by Ben and Mary Griffin, a physician and his wife, but it had originally belonged to the Shy family, eight members of whom were buried in the cemetery. Mary Griffin had called the police when she noticed that the grave of Civil War veteran lieutenant colonel William Shy had been disturbed. The grass had been removed from the plot, and a 3-foot (1m) hole had been dug. Deputies first assumed that vandals had been searching for Civil War artifacts, such as swords and medals. That notion vanished, however, when they saw a headless corpse, barely covered with freshly turned earth, laying atop

the original coffin. Obviously a murder had been committed. The perpetrators had planned to bury their victim in a ready-made grave, but had been scared away.

Bass had retrieved plenty of bodies from graves in his career as a forensic anthropologist. During the 1950s, he had carried out archaeological work for the Smithsonian Institution, excavating and analyzing Native American remains in South Dakota. He had been mentored by renowned anthropologist Charles E. Snow, who took him out on his first forensic case, and by Wilton Krogman, an internationally acclaimed "bone detective." (The term *forensic anthropologist* was not recognized by the scientific community until 1972.) Thus, Bass was confident of his skills as he joined law enforcement officials who were gathered in the rain, eyeing the corpse that lay mostly covered with muddy earth.

The murder had obviously taken place some time before; a pungent odor of decay told everyone that the victim was

Skeletal remains at an Indian burial ground in Delaware. Early in his career, forensic anthropologist William Bass excavated and analyzed Native American remains in South Dakota.

decomposing. Unbothered by the smell, Bass laid out a piece of plywood on which to place the body, then began carefully removing the dirt. As the hole got deeper, he climbed down inside with his feet on either side of the corpse so he could fully uncover it. "Counting my excavations of Indian burials in the Great Plains, I've been in somewhere around five thousand graves," he recalls. "By the time I die I suspect I'll hold some sort of unofficial record: 'body that's been in and out of the most graves ever.'"[6]

Becoming a Forensic Anthropologist

Job Description:
Forensic anthropologists help identify unknown bodies or body parts and skeletal remains and determine the estimated time since death and cause of death. Work is carried out both in the lab and in the field. The work involves exposure to potentially dangerous and disturbing situations.

Education:
Aspiring forensic anthropologists must first earn a bachelor of arts degree (BA) in anthropology from a four-year college, then a master of arts (MA) degree in anthropology, followed by a doctor of philosophy (PhD) degree in anthropology. Once their education is completed, forensic anthropologists should achieve board certification by the American Board of Forensic Anthropology.

Qualifications:
Aspiring forensic anthropologists must be objective, persistent, and enjoy solving puzzles. They must be able to handle situations involving death and decay.

Salary:
$40,000 to $100,000 per year

A Quick Assessment

Once the body was uncovered, Bass saw that it had decayed to the point that the legs were separated from the pelvis and the arms were detached from the shoulders. Carefully, he handed the remains to deputies who placed them in anatomical order to resemble a complete body on the plywood. When Bass was finished, the entire corpse—except for the head—was laid out before them. Despite the dirt, everyone could see that it was dressed in a formal black suit, black vest, pleated white shirt, and dress shoes. Bass remembers, "I wondered if the victim had been a waiter from some fancy Nashville or Franklin restaurant. Either that or a groomsman at a wedding."[7]

Part of the coffin lid had broken inward, so Bass poked his head in to see if the skull had fallen inside. It was not there, and he also noted that nothing was left of the late colonel Shy but small piles of disintegrated rubble. He was not surprised. Bodies rotted away quickly in Tennessee's damp earth, and Colonel Shy had been in the ground over one hundred years.

With the retrieval complete, Bass placed the remains in bags and put them in the trunk of his car. A careful methodical worker, he planned to analyze them in his lab in Knoxville over the next few days. Deputies were anxious to get an estimate of time of death in order to begin their investigation, however, so he made a quick assessment. He looked at the still-pink tissue and remnants of organs in the body cavity and stated: "It appears the man has been dead two months to a year. … A year may be a little too much."[8] The story of the discovery soon made the news, and Bass's estimate was printed in the *Nashville Banner*, along with a quote from deputy Fleming Williams, who said, "It looks like we have a homicide on our hands."[9]

Identifying the Mystery Man

Over the next few days, Bass studied the body more closely. The bones told him that he was looking at a young male in his mid-twenties, about 5-feet, 10-inches (1.8m) tall. That was reasonable; many modern murder victims are young males.

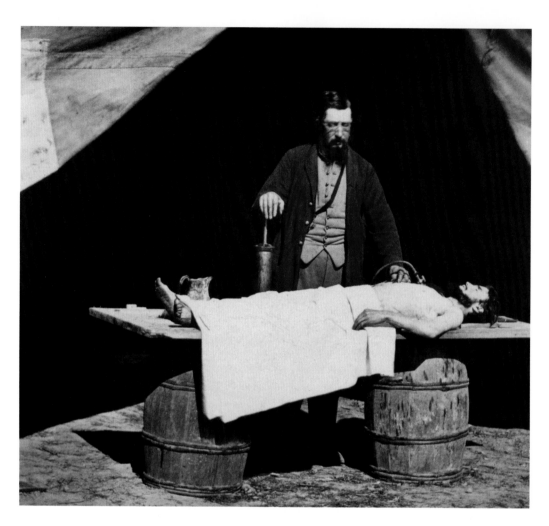

A doctor embalms a dead Civil War soldier. Forensic expert William Bass started his body farm practice after failing to recognize that a presumed murder victim was actually the well-preserved body of a Civil War veteran.

After another search of the coffin revealed that the rubble was the victim's skull, including teeth. The skull's shattered condition made it clear that he had been killed by a very large projectile. "Our mystery man had died a violent, instantaneous death,"[10] Bass decided.

While those clues were easy for the forensic expert to explain, others were more puzzling. Following standard procedures, Bass had simmered the remains in a pot of water to soften and remove the tissue from the bones. Oddly, the simmering remains gave off a chemical smell, rather than the straightforward stench of cooked flesh, indicating that the body had been embalmed (preserved with chemicals to prevent decay). Bass knew of no murderers who ever took the time to do that. In addition, although the victim had been well dressed, his teeth had many cavities, and one showed signs of an absess. The lack of dental work in an apparently well-off man was also odd. The conflicting evidence made Bass uneasy. He started to wonder if the case was really a modern-day murder as everyone had first assumed.

A phone call from a perplexed crime technician added to his unease. The labels in the dead man's clothing could not be traced to any known manufacturer. The fibers were all natural—cotton and silk—and the lacing up the trouser legs was totally unique, as if they came from a different era. The man's shoes were unique, too. The technician finally asked if the body could be that of Colonel Shy, and Bass had to face his doubts head on.

As embarrassing as it was to admit, it made sense that the body was that of Shy. Dentistry had been primitive in the Civil War era. Embalming was not common at that time, but a well-to-do family like the Shys would have been able to afford it. They would have buried the colonel in his best clothes, too, and would also have been able to afford the top-of-the-line, well-sealed coffin that lay in the grave. Made of cast iron mixed with lead, it had protected the body from moisture, and the lead had acted as a preservative. That would explain the still-pink flesh on Shy's bones.

A quick check with local historians confirmed that William Shy had been twenty-six when he died. He had been killed by a large, soft bullet called a minié ball in the Battle of Nashville in 1864. The ball had traveled in a downward arc, striking Shy's skull from above so forcefully that it had fractured it into seventeen pieces. The mystery of the headless corpse was solved.

New Insight

When local newsmen learned of Bass's inaccurate analysis, they quickly called him with questions. Specifically, they wanted to know how he had mistaken a Civil War corpse for a recent murder victim. Bass explained that the body had been exceptionally well preserved. It had also looked like it had been dumped into the grave, not pulled out of a hole in the top of the coffin. Taking the two circumstances together, he and the deputies had assumed they were looking at a recent murder victim. "I got the age, sex, race, height and weight right," he told a reporter from the *Nashville Banner*. "But I was off on the time of death by 113 years."[11]

The incident held enough human interest to be picked up by the Associated Press wire service, and the story of Colonel Shy made newspapers worldwide. Readers learned that one of the most respected forensic specialists in the United States had made a stupendous error. They wondered why he had not known better. Bass was red faced, but he was asking himself the same thing. He had had a fine education and a great deal of experience working with human remains. He was considered an expert by his scientific peers and by law enforcement officials. Yet his miscalculation made it obvious that he knew too little about human decomposition. And that was because there was little mention of it in academic literature. Scientists had studied animal decomposition, and pathologists had documented changes such as rigor mortis (stiffening of the body), algor mortis (decline in body temperature), and livor mortis (discoloring of parts of the body) that occurred in humans in the hours immediately after death. But the entire process of human decay had never been studied, primarily because social customs and religious beliefs had discouraged research.

Bass realized that if any good was to come from his blunder, he would have to break taboos and tackle the subject himself. Over the next months, he formulated a plan. He would study human corpses in-depth in order to be better able to determine the postmortem interval (PMI). PMI is all-important, because if time of death is known, police are better able to know the period of time they should be investigating, whether that is just a few days or many years in the past. Knowing time of death could also help police trace a victim's last movements,

The Postmortem Interval

The postmortem interval (PMI) is the period of time between death and discovery of the body. A number of medical and scientific techniques, based on changes that occur to the body, can be used to determine the PMI. Some of those changes include:

- algor mortis: A steady decline in body temperature that begins immediately after death and continues until body temperature matches air temperature, usually within two hours.

- rigor mortis: A chemical change in the muscles after death resulting in a stiffening of the arms and legs. It can be used to determine the PMI until stiffening passes, usually in about thirty-six hours.

- livor mortis: Discoloration caused by the settling or pooling of blood into portions of the body closest to the ground. It can be used to help determine PMI up to twelve hours after death.

- the vitreous humor: The clear gel that fills the space between the lens and the retina of the eyeball. It dries out after death. This happens fairly quickly, so it can be used to determine the PMI only in the early stages of death.

- decomposition: Predictable changes in the body that start almost immediately after death and last up to a year. Identifying a corpse's stage of decomposition can allow the PMI to be determined within a range of several hours.

discover the last people to see him or her alive, and identify possible suspects.

A Facility Unlike Any Other in the World

As head of the Department of Anthropology at the University of Tennessee, Bass was in a good position to tackle human decomposition research. He had several faculty members

The remains of two bodies lie in the woods near the Anthropology Research Facility at the University of Tennessee in Knoxville. The bodies are placed on grounds in different types of situations to see how the bodies will decompose.

working in his department, and graduate students were willing and able to help carry out the projects he envisioned. He remembers,

> We had ... resources to do something that had never been done before: to establish a research facility unlike any other in the world—a research facility that would

systematically study human bodies by the dozens; …
a laboratory where nature would be allowed to take its
course with mortal flesh under a variety of experimen-
tal conditions. At every step, scientists and graduate
students would observe the processes … and chart the
timing of human decomposition.[12]

"Beloved by Everyone"

*Described as jolly, jaunty, and perpetually cheerful, William M. Bass
retains his optimism and scientific curiosity despite personal sorrow. In
the excerpt below from the article "Questions from the Grave," author
Karen Collins explains:*

Along with the highs of career successes, Bass has faced the
lows of personal loss—he lost two wives to cancer. Ann, his wife
of 40 years, died in 1993. … Bass's second wife, Annette, died
of cancer 3 years after they married. [Third wife] Carol Bass
was a childhood playmate who lived near Bass's grandfather in
Lynchburg, Virginia. The couple … celebrated their eighth an-
niversary [in 2006].

Bass's colleagues say optimism and humility are his most outstand-
ing traits. "He will help anyone who asks, he will perform any
service requested of him, and he will ask nothing in return," said
UT [University of Tennessee]'s [Mike] Sullivan. "Bill Bass is one of
the most honorable, ethical, and personable human beings I have
ever met. He is beloved by everyone who has ever met him, and
the reasons are (immediately) obvious. He has a quick smile, a
ready humor, and he is always willing to share his knowledge with
anyone who is interested."

Karen Collins, "Questions from the Grave," *Tennessee Alumnus Magazine*, Spring 2006,
http://pr.tennessee.edu/alumnus/alumarticle.asp?id=668.

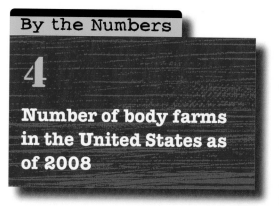

Despite his new resolve, Bass was not sure that he could get the university to support his efforts. He and journalist Jon Jefferson explain, "The idea was simple; the implications—and the possible complications—were profound. By most cultural standards and values, such research could appear gruesome, disrespectful, even shocking."[13] His enthusiasm and vision were infectious and convincing, however. Jefferson observes: "The thing about Dr. Bass that's so great is that he's able to take this macabre subject and get you so fascinated…. You get caught up in his view that this is a scientific puzzle, an effort to uncover the truth. Ultimately, it's a quest for justice."[14]

Chancellor Jack Reese felt the same. He did not question the wisdom of the project and offered Bass a small plot of unused land behind the university's medical center as a work site. The land was not prime real estate—the hospital's trash had been dumped there until environmental regulations put an end to outdoor burning. But Bass was satisfied.

Body 1-81

With land and a vision, Bass began his project in 1980. Neither he nor his students were skilled laborers, but they cut back the brush in the middle of the site, hauled in gravel, smoothed it, and then poured a 16 square foot (1.5sq. m) slab of concrete. On the back of the slab, they built a small shed where they could store tools, instruments, and supplies such as shovels, scalpels, and latex gloves. The front part of the slab was left exposed so that they could lay out the bodies they would study. Around the slab they ran a chain-link fence with a locked gate. They also ran electricity and water lines from the medical center, and built a gravel driveway for delivery trucks to come and go. Bass and Jefferson point out, "People who know the Body Farm today seem to think it sprang into existence fully formed, but that's not the way it happened. It came from humble beginnings, and it progressed by small steps."[15]

While the site was being prepared, Bass sent out letters of inquiry to medical examiners and funeral directors throughout Tennessee, asking for corpses for his experiment. Responses were slow, but one body became available in May 1981. On a Thursday evening Bass drove his covered pickup truck to the Burris Funeral Home in Crossville, Tennessee, one hour west of Knoxville. A woman had agreed to donate the body of her seventy-three-year-old father who had died of alcoholism, emphysema, and heart disease, on the condition that his identity be kept confidential.

Bass had already decided that the identity of all his subjects would remain secret. To ensure that, he adopted a simple but unique identification code. The first donation of 1981 was known as 1-81. The second to arrive in 1981 would be 2-81 and so forth. Bass and his students respectfully placed 1-81 on the concrete pad they had built, took several photos, and covered him with a wire mesh cage to keep away rodents and other predators. As Bass and Jefferson write of that moment, "death's acre was open for business. The Body Farm was born."[16]

Serious Work

Despite Bass's acceptance and use of the term *body farm*, the name offended other serious researchers who saw it as inaccurate and flippant. It caught the public's fancy, however, and became an established term for the facility and others like it. "Initially, I objected to the term 'Body Farm,'" explains Floyd (Jerry) Melbye, founder of Texas State University's facility, "but two things have changed my mind. First, we have not come up with an accurate substitute term, and second, it has become universally accepted by the public and scientists alike."[17]

With publicity came calls from everyone from international journalists to Cub Scout den mothers, asking for a tour. Bass accepted few requests because he believed that it would not be appropriate for the curious to wander among the bodies, gaping and taking pictures. "This is a research facility with which we're

Texas State University body farm founder Jerry Melbye moves a mummy into position during an examination of 111 mummies found in Guanajuato, Mexico in 2007.

trying to help police, morticians and society. It's not a tourist attraction,"[18] he points out.

As a research facility, the Body Farm in Tennessee soon became a prestigious learning institution, where the most dedicated scientists came to study. New body farms are held in similar high esteem. Admittance into their graduate programs is difficult; applicants must have at least a 3.8 grade point average in prior class work, higher than that required to get into medical school. Even then, there are usually waiting lists. Texas State accepted only nine students into its first class. In Tennessee, fewer than 10 percent of applicants get in. Those who are accepted are well aware of the unique opportunity they have been given. "I packed up or sold everything I had … to study under Dr. Bass. He's got an international reputation,"[19] says Emily Craig, who went on to become a forensic anthropologist for the Kentucky Medical Examiner's Office after studying at the Body Farm.

Although prestigious, the small, unkempt plots of ground where the work is carried out are a far cry from the sterile, well-equipped rooms that ordinarily come to mind when the word *laboratory* is mentioned. By definition, body farms are insect infested, foul smelling, grim, and disturbing. Nevertheless, a walk through them also reveals them to be some of the most fascinating scientific establishments in the world.

CHAPTER 2

Death's Acres

William M. Bass's Anthropology Research Facility had only recently been established when the professor began talking about the need for similar facilities in other locales. Bodies decay differently in different environments, so Bass and his colleagues believed that decomposition information was needed for each part of the country. Ideally, there would be at least one body farm in each state, so that law enforcement would have experts at hand who were familiar with decomposition under local conditions. "The goal of law enforcement and the criminal justice system is to take … offenders off the street," says forensic expert Jason Byrd. "You can't expect (them) to do that without the proper tools."[20]

Not in My Backyard

Although supporters see body farms as important to society and law enforcement, most proposals to create more body farms are rejected for a variety of reasons. First, many people shrink from thinking about death and dying. Then, many are horrified at the thought of bodies being treated disrespectfully. For religious and moral reasons, they object to leaving a body in the open air where it will be torn apart and eaten by insects and animals. So even if community leaders see the value of the research, they hesitate to say so for fear they will lose support and/or be voted out of office.

In addition to being perceived as disrespectful, body farms are also perceived by some as unnecessary luxuries. The research is not judged to be worth the several million dollars it takes to start a body farm. In Nevada, a proposed facility near Las Vegas was not built because neither government nor

Clark County, Nevada, coroner Michael Murphy removes flowers from a casket during an exhumation. Murphy is in favor of plans for a body farm near Las Vegas, but funding has not yet come through.

university officials would come up with money to equip it. Forensic experts had cited its importance not only for law enforcement but also because the climate and terrain is similar to that of the Middle East. By studying death in Nevada, researchers hoped to better understand death on modern-day battlefields, in places like Iraq and Afghanistan. Clark County, Nevada, coroner Michael Murphy thinks the facility will be created one day. "I'm the eternal optimist," he says. "I believe there is a very strong possibility that it could happen. That it will happen."[21]

Finally, there are people who acknowledge the value of body farms, but do not want one in their neighborhood. For instance, Chico State University administrators discourage efforts by anthropology professor Turhon Murad and others to create one in Northern California, arguing that there is no appropriate locale for one in their urban community. In Youngstown, Ohio, university administrators rejected a proposal made by the Ohio Bureau of Criminal Identification and Investigation after more than 150 people turned out to protest, citing possible health risks and declining property values. Dean John Yemma stated, "We will not move forward with any plans without the full support of the residents of the area."[22]

NIMBY

NIMBY is an acronym for "not in my backyard." It describes the outrage and opposition expressed by members of a community when they learn that something they do not want, such as a landfill or a body farm, has been proposed for their neighborhood. In the following excerpt from the article "NIMBY," author Peter M. Sandman explains the basis of a community's outrage:

Imagine pulling into your driveway after a long day's work and noticing that there are strangers picnicking in your back yard. "Get out of my back yard!" you demand. "Why?" they inquire. "We've done a site analysis. Your back yard is a prime location for our picnic. And we've done a risk assessment. Our picnic is unlikely to do any significant permanent damage to your back yard." They didn't ask your permission; they didn't invite you to the picnic; they won't even tell you exactly what they're eating. Odds are you're pretty steamed. Even if they're right about the substantive issues, even if you realize the risk to your back yard is actually minimal, you're still pretty steamed.

Of course in this example it's literally your back yard. You have a legal right to forbid trespassing on your property. The principle is slightly different when it's not quite your back yard; it's the developer's property but your neighborhood, your community. But the feeling of being invaded by outsiders is much the same.

Peter M. Sandman, "NIMBY," SAGE, February 17, 2008, www.psandman.com/col/nimby.htm.

Real Concerns

Planners faced public complaints when they first chose a location for Western Carolina's body farm, so they downplayed their second choice in hopes of avoiding further objections. In a letter to nearby landowners, the facility was called a "forensics research station" and no mention was made of the corpses that would be decaying there. Residents soon guessed the truth, however, and again complained. "I'm wondering how half a dozen bodies strewn about land near my house would benefit

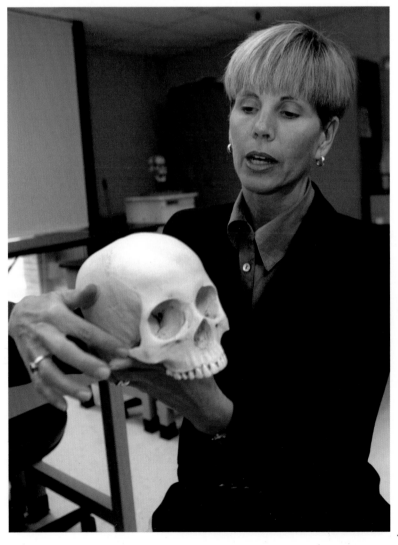

Forensics anthropologist Joan Bytheway demonstrates observation techniques used in determining gender with a human skull replica. She is part of the faculty at Sam Houston State University College of Criminal Justice, where a new body farm is in the works.

me in the long run? I think I'd rather have a nice new landfill or maybe even a spiffy nudie bar [strip club] down the road from my abode [house],"[23] wrote journalist Susan Reinhardt.

Planners at Texas State University in San Marcos also had to overcome objections before they could set up their body farm. Their first proposed site was near a strip mall and drew protests from area residents who feared the odor from the facility would befoul their shopping spaces. The next proposed site near an airport caused aviation officials to worry that vultures circling over the facility would get sucked into the engines of jets taking off or landing, and cause crashes.

Planners at Sam Houston State University avoided controversy by keeping their facility secret in its initial planning stages. The site is in the middle of university land that has long been used to study topics relating to decomposition in animals, so administrators, who broke ground on the project in August 2008, hope that complaints will always be minimal. "I think we'll probably get a little bit of backlash from the public, but I think when they know we're going to handle it with dignity and the utmost respect, they'll find it OK,"[24] says anthropology professor Joan Bytheway. Bytheway conceived of the facility in 2005 while excavating mass graves in Iraq.

Small But Well Protected

Because of tight budgets and unpopularity, existing body farms are necessarily small. The Tennessee facility is set on a 2.5-acre (1ha) wooded plot, although in 2007 the university promised another 12 to 15 acres (5ha–6ha) for its future use. North Carolina's facility is the size of a garage and is able to hold only six bodies at a time. In Texas, Sam Houston State University's facility will encompass only 1 acre (0.4ha), while Texas State's facility is 5 acres (2ha), the largest in the world. Planners hope it will eventually include a pond so that decay in water can be studied.

In addition to being small, body farms are placed in secluded locales, although they must be close enough to a university and an airport so that researchers and visiting law enforcement can easily get to them. Only the well-informed find the Tennessee facility beyond the employee parking lot of the University Medical Center. In North Carolina the Forensic Osteology Research Station (FOREST) is located outside the small town of Cullowhee in the center of an undeveloped 344-acre (139ha) tract of land, at least 0.5 mile (0.8km) from any residential building. Texas State's is located well inside the boundaries of 3,000-acre (1,214ha) Freeman Ranch, 5 miles (8km) west of San Marcos, while Sam Houston State University's in Huntsville is on a dead-end road with the nearest home more than 1 mile (1.6km) away.

> ## By the Numbers
>
> ## 400
>
> **Approximate number of bodies that have decayed at the Body Farm in Tennessee**

Although new facilities are private, experience has proven that they still need to be well protected. Before setting up the Body Farm, Bass worked cases for local law enforcement, and stored victims' bodies in a vacant cow barn on land owned by the university. A minimum-security prison for nonviolent offenders was nearby, however, and inmates worked on the grounds near the barn. Bass soon noticed footprints inside, a sure sign that his grisly subjects had attracted curious visitors. Sometimes the corpses were disarranged, too, proving that they were vulnerable to theft or vandalism. He remembers, "Nothing had been removed, but I didn't want to take a chance of losing a crucial piece of forensic evidence—a skull or a telltale bullet, for instance."[25]

Shortly thereafter, Bass moved his subjects to the site of the present Body Farm. Despite two fences, fraternity pranksters and Halloween vandals still managed to get inside, so he topped the fences with razor wire and installed video cameras around the perimeter. Even those precautions did not completely stop trespassers, some of whom were seriously cut when they tried to get over the wire.

Taking a lesson from Bass's difficulties, Western Carolina administrators do not publicize the exact location of their body farm to discourage curiosity seekers and intruders. They have also surrounded the facility with two fences, trees, and vegetation. The Texas body farms are equipped with razor wire, electric fences, motion sensors, infrared lights, and security cameras. At Freeman Ranch, all visitors must check in at headquarters and three security cards are needed to get through the gates of the outdoor lab itself.

Outdoor Laboratories

Behind the protective fences, the outdoor labs are the spaces that give body farms their gruesome reputation. Bodies are positioned here and there, apparently at random, although the location of each one is carefully documented. Each has a plastic tag strapped to an arm and an ankle. The tags identify its ethnicity, sex, age, and order of arrival. For instance "WF 30 3/95" would indicate that a subject is a white female, thirty years old, and the third body to be placed in the outdoor lab in 1995. Each body is accessed by rough paths made by the researchers' regular visits. Such visits are carefully documented to maintain a chain of custody, chronological documentation showing who worked with the body, what was done and/or observed, and when. Thus, if facts learned during decomposition are used in legal cases, no questions can be raised about their authenticity or accuracy.

Because it is the purpose of outdoor labs to mimic environmental conditions under which corpses decay, some bodies are positioned in open spaces where the sun is intense. Others are in shady areas. Some are on grass, some are buried under concrete. A few decay out of sight in hiding places that murderers often choose—an oil drum, a trash bin, or a car trunk. "What you'll see here is what's going to be happening at a real crime scene,"[26] says researcher Arpad Vass.

Bodies are in all stages of decomposition. The freshest look startlingly lifelike. Others are bloated and discolored, swarming with flies and churning with masses of larvae, known as maggots. Those that have been outdoors for several weeks are little more than brown skin and bones and tend to blend into the earth. In the autumn, rain and dead leaves cover them. In winter, they are blanketed with snow. Most are left untouched until they skeletonize. Journalist Terry Moseley writes of the Tennessee facility: "The farm is a morbid hybrid of serene woodland and violent crime scene. The silence is unsettling as you walk through … land littered with exposed cadavers and body bags with an occasional decaying limb peeking out."[27]

Chain-of-Custody Guidelines

Chain of custody is the documented transfer of evidence from person to person from the moment the evidence is collected. This written record, arranged in order of date and time, lists who had control of the evidence and when. Police, crime scene investigators, and lab personnel follow chain-of-custody guidelines to ensure that evidence is not lost or tampered with and to prevent any misconduct, situations that can compromise a case in court. The guidelines are:

- Keep the number of people involved in collecting and handling evidence and documentation to a minimum.
- Only allow people associated with the case to handle the evidence and documentation.
- Always use proper chain-of-custody forms to document the transfer of evidence from person to person.
- Clearly and legibly identify evidence, fill out forms, and complete documentation using permanent ink.

The Smell of Death

Odor is an ever-present reality in outdoor labs. The smell of decomposition is especially strong during hot weather and is so repulsive that it makes some visitors vomit. It is often described as sickeningly sweet. Others say it is a putrid combination of rancid butter, rotten meat, and poorly serviced portable toilets. No matter what it suggests, it clings to clothes and hair and is difficult to eliminate. "It can really challenge the gag reflex," remarks researcher and University of Tennessee (UT) faculty member Murray Marks. "But you learn to breathe through your mouth, and you get used to it."[28]

Flies are everywhere, too, swarming in clouds over fresh bodies and researchers, looking for food and moist places to lay their eggs. Bass and journalist Jon Jefferson write about the hardships endured by student William Rodriguez, who carried out some of the first insect studies in 1981. "Sitting just

Part of the natural decomposition process includes the presence of such predators as crows, vultures, raccoons, rats, and maggots. Here, vultures feast on corpses at a murder scene.

a foot or two away from a bloody body, Bill would soon find even himself overrun with flies, seeking … any dark, damp orifices (including Bill's nostrils) to lay their eggs in. He quickly learned to wrap netting around his head to keep the flies out of his eyes, nose, mouth, and ears."[29] Flies leave once a body dries, but then there are other insects with which to cope. "I thought there would be a lot of flies and bugs, but all there was around was bees,"[30] says crime scene technician Dale Allison of his visit.

In addition to insects, larger predators visit the premises. Crows and vultures may descend for a quick meal during the

Quick and Dirty

One of the first experiments William M. Bass carried out at the Body Farm was inspired by the discovery of a badly decayed corpse in a vacant lot on a busy Knoxville street in 1976. Neither neighbors nor passersby had noticed a smell of decay, and Bass wondered why. "If the human nose couldn't detect a body at that distance, at which distance *could* it detect a decomposing corpse? The answer would be useful not just to me … but to police, firefighters, and search-and-rescue workers."

To get an answer, Bass took one of his donated subjects that was bloated and foul smelling and hid it behind bushes and trees in a far corner of the Body Farm. He placed markers at 10-yard (9m) intervals on the route leading to the corpse. He then led a group of students along the route, instructing them to tell him when they smelled something. The students did not react until they were between 10 and 20 yards (9m–18m) from the body. Bass noted, "The research was quick and dirty … but it was good enough to show me that yes, you *can* die and decompose in a vacant lot … and never be smelled by thousands of people passing by just fifty feet away."

Bill Bass and Jon Jefferson, *Death's Acre*, New York: Berkeley, 2003, pp. 117–18.

day, while raccoons and rats feast on maggots and carry away small bones at night. Infrared cameras with motion detectors capture images of the night visitors, and researchers use their activities to learn to distinguish tooth marks from injuries made by murderers. "We're always interested in separating human action from animal action,"[31] says Richard Jantz, director of the Forensic Anthropology Center in Tennessee.

Indoor Labs

After the corpses are reduced to bones, they are transferred to indoor laboratories to be cleaned, examined, documented, and stored. At the Body Farm, the indoor labs were housed for years in an unused dormitory built under Neyland Stadium where football games took place every fall.

Beginning in 1999, however, autopsies (examinations of corpses to determine cause of death), bone processing, and other research is carried out in the new William M. Bass Forensic Anthropology Lab that adjoins the UT Medical Center. The lab is equipped with a large walk-in cooler, a modern ventilation system, computers, and the like. "This is fancy. They thought of everything,"[32] says former Knox County medical examiner Sandra Elkins. The Western Carolina Human Identification Laboratory in North Carolina is also modern and equipped to carry out everything from the removal of soft tissue from bone to the analysis of cremated remains. At the Texas State University body farm, a new 1-million-dollar lab is under construction.

Flies and the smell of decay are common in indoor labs, but overall the spaces are much more clean and orderly than outdoors. There are a variety of kettles, saws, brushes, and tweezers for removing decayed flesh from bone. There are refrigerators and freezers to preserve remains, examining tables for studying them, and microscopes for analyzing tissue and bone at the cellular level. In these labs, workers piece broken bones together, take measurements, and prepare skeletons for storage. Here, too, they also carry out experiments that cannot be done outdoors, such as categorizing saw marks, making microscopic studies of bones that are burned or otherwise injured, and identifying unknown victims. Maintaining the chain of command is still a priority, and every step of each activity is carefully documented so that the work will be seen as valid if it is used in criminal cases later.

Body Farm Residents

In order for work to be carried out on body farms, researchers need a continuous supply of corpses. In 1980, the year Bass opened his facility, only four became available. In subsequent years numbers increased, and subjects were mainly vagrants or unidentified crime victims such as a woman who was found floating in the Tennessee River, or a man who appeared to be a victim of a drug deal gone wrong. By the year 2000 there were still vagrants and a few people who committed suicide, but many subjects are persons whose bodies have been donated by family members. A growing number are individuals who specifically directed that their bodies go to the facilities after death. They come from throughout the United States, and make up a diverse group ranging from judges to schoolteachers.

Roy Crawford, a fifty-four-year-old mining engineer from Kentucky, will be one of them. He decided to donate his body

Body farms are always in need of corpses and body parts so that researchers can continue their studies. Here, human skulls line a shelf at the forensic anthropology lab at Western Carolina University.

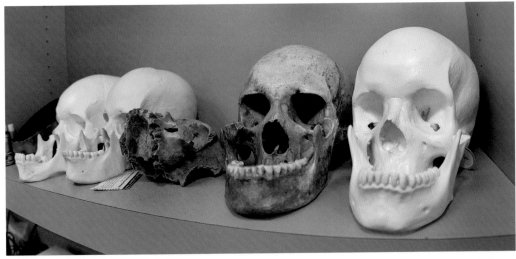

after he dies for several reasons. "I like the idea that one day research done on my body might be used to catch a murderer," he says. "I [also] look at the [body farm] as a scientific laboratory in nature, and I think nature is beautiful. The idea of being propped up against a tree to decompose sounds a whole lot better than being locked in a box and preserved under the ground."[33]

Donations are permanent unless family members change their mind and request a return. There is no cost to donate, although those who live some distance away are responsible for arranging and paying for transportation to the facility. All facilities provide donation forms which can be filled out and submitted. Medical histories are requested, so researchers can look for and document the physical effects of cancer, heart disease, injuries, and the like. A photograph is requested as well, so that forensic artists who reconstruct facial features from skulls can sharpen their skills. Individuals who have contracted HIV/AIDS, hepatitis, tuberculosis, or antibiotic-resistant bacterial infections are not accepted due to the danger of infecting researchers. The University of Tennessee accepts thirty to fifty donations per year and has over one thousand people on file to donate in the future. "The presumption that it is insulting or demeaning to donate your body is false. It is a final gift to the living,"[34] says Floyd (Jerry) Melbye, founder of Texas State University's facility.

Those who donate their bodies often imagine themselves decaying in a peaceful spot such as under a shady tree with a view of the Tennessee River, or behind the wheel of a white Cadillac convertible that has seen better days. In fact, though, no one can say where their body will be placed, or of what project they will be a part. They can be sure, however, that no matter where their remains are situated, they will be treated with as much respect as any living person. Marks says, "I cannot divorce myself from the fact that I am the caretaker of these people. I respect this incredibly precious gift."[35]

CHAPTER 3

Swarming with Insects

When the Body Farm in Tennessee opened in 1981, anthropology professor William M. Bass and his graduate students were looking for answers to simple questions. Researcher Rebecca Wilson says those questions were "how [do] … we decompose? What do we look like at different stages of decomposition? If I have a body that's been dead for three days, what does that look like and can I tell you it's been dead for three days?"[36]

To find answers they began by watching and documenting every change that a body underwent, from how long it took the first fly to arrive to when the corpse became completely skeletonized. After learning the basics, they went on to tackle more complex unknowns. They studied the climate's effect on decay. They studied decay in conditions similar to those found in real murder cases. They also carried out groundbreaking research involving insects and their vital role in the decomposition process. Bass states, "There are a lot of factors that can affect how a body decomposes, but we found that the major two are climate and insects."[37]

The Decomposition Process

The first step in learning about human decomposition involved observing the corpse as it decayed. The task was simple but time-consuming. From the moment a subject was placed in the outdoor lab, someone was assigned to watch it, photograph it, and record every detail of the changes that occurred. Observation had to take place almost nonstop in the beginning because decomposition progresses very quickly. Researchers did not want to miss a single detail that might be significant.

As part of a body's decomposition process, fatty tissues break down under the skin to give it a glossy shine, as seen in this picture.

Later, the corpse was visited every day or two because changes occurred more slowly.

Students who had never seen a decaying body before were often repulsed and sickened when they began the observation process. They soon adjusted, however, to disconcerting sights such as wasps crawling in and out of a subject's mouth or crows tearing at a subject's intestines. They also came to accept death and decay as ugly but natural processes from which much could be learned. Forensic anthropologist and former Body Farm student Emily Craig remembers, "Somehow, the shocking had come commonplace, and the human remains I saw rotting in the sun had begun to look more like three-dimensional puzzles and less like once-living human beings."[38] Soon, instead of gagging and vomiting, the students were able to watch the movement of thousands of squirming maggots as they disarrayed clothing, making it seem like the corpse had been searched when in fact, it had not. They noted that decompositional fluids seeped from the body, destroying all vegetation under the corpse and staining the ground black. They saw larger predators scatter and carry away bones, leaving confusing results for law enforcement officials to decipher.

The most significant observations were of the decay process itself. Under all but the most extreme conditions, it occurred

The Body at Death

In order to completely understand human decomposition, forensic scientists must understand the living body and how anatomical processes shutdown at death. That shutdown progresses as follows:

1 The heart stops beating and the lungs stop breathing.

2 Body cells no longer receive supplies of blood and oxygen.

3 Cells cease aerobic respiration [which relies on an intake of oxygen] and do not generate the energy molecules needed to maintain normal function.

4 Cells eventually die and the body loses its capacity to fight off bacteria.

5 The cells' enzymes and bacterial activity cause the body to begin to decompose.

in a predictable progression, the first stage of which Bass calls the "fresh" phase. This begins about four minutes after death and ends when the body becomes visibly bloated. During the fresh phase, the corpse resembles an unconscious, living person. Despite being fresh, however, it attracts flies, which lay eggs in wounds and body openings. The eggs hatch into thousands of maggots which begin consuming the flesh. At the same time, bacteria in the intestines invade other parts of the body and start breaking down tissues.

Breakdown

As bacteria attack the body, gases such as hydrogen sulfide, methane, cadaverine, and putrescine are produced inside the corpse, and it enters the second, or "bloat" phase. It swells to grotesque proportions and the skin takes on a rich, reddish-brown color. Fatty tissues break down under the skin and give

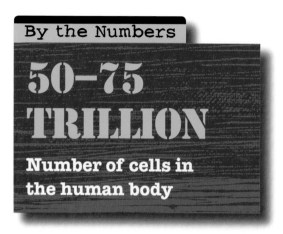

it a glossy shine, as if it has been glazed. Arteries, veins, and capillaries become visible as purplish-crimson lines, similar to rivers on a map. Eventually the skin splits and sloughs off in large sheets. Maggots eat away large portions of flesh, creating gaping holes.

The "decay" stage follows bloating. At this point the combination of maggot and bacterial activity finally breaks down skin and flesh enough so the body deflates, leaving the belly shrunken and the rib cage jutting upward. Tissue grows soft, decomposition fluids ooze into the soil, and the gut-wrenching smell of decay becomes extremely strong. Bass observes, "I have noted a strong correlation between the onset of the Decay Stage and a rise in absences and sick days among my graduate students."[39] By the end of the decay stage, 80 percent of the corpse has decomposed away, leaving mostly skin and bone behind.

Bass calls the final stage of decomposition the "dry" stage, although some experts consider this same period to be two stages: "postdecay" and "skeletal." During postdecay, remains are dry and any remaining skin and hair on the skeleton is slowly eaten by insects. During the skeletal stage—the latter part of Bass's dry stage—the bones break down. Heat, water, and acids in the soil cause organic material to leach away, and brittle minerals that remain eventually crumble to dust.

A Decomposition Timeline

At the same time that Bass and his students became familiar with every observable change produced by decomposition, they timed the changes. In Tennessee, a body was fresh for no more than three days; bloating could last from day four to day ten; the decay stage generally lasted to day twenty; and postdecay up until about day fifty. The skeletal phase was the longest and could continue up to a year or more, although at body farms, researchers end this phase within several months. "Normally

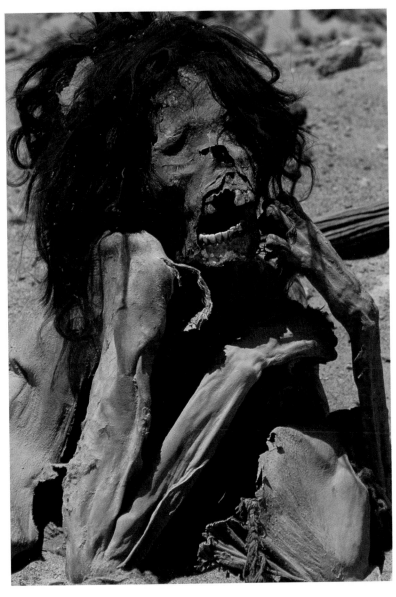

Climate and environment are two key factors in how fast or slow a body decomposes. Bodies found in hot, dry locations, such as the body shown here, often retain their skin and hair, and appear more like mummies than skeletons.

we don't leave a body out there longer than a year because then the sun begins to bleach them [the bones] and they'll crack,"[40] explains Bass.

Bass knew that his decomposition timeline was variable, however. Experience had taught him that climate, environment, and insect activity interacted to speed or slow the process. Bodies found in hot, dry locales such as Nevada, for instance, dry so fast that the bloat and decay stages are virtually absent. The result is not a skeleton, but a mummified victim with flesh and skin intact. In contrast, bodies found on a Kansas prairie rapidly decay to clean bones. "Kansas corpses tended to be clean, sun-bleached skeletons, like something you see in a Hollywood western,"[41] Bass and journalist Jon Jefferson explain.

Before establishing the Body Farm, Bass and other forensic experts had only guessed at factors that caused differences in decay. They presumed that bodies were more likely to become maggot infested in Tennessee, for instance, because humidity and vegetation produced large insect populations. But they did not know for sure if this was true. Now they set out to learn exactly how insect activity, climate, and environment worked together so that variations could be explained. When body farms were established in North Carolina and Texas, researchers in those facilities began to do the same for their parts of the country, too.

Faunal Succession

The field of forensic entomology—the study of insects as they relate to crime—was badly overlooked by experts over the years. In fact, prior to the 1990s, if law enforcement officials found maggots on a body at a crime scene, they washed them away before conducting an autopsy. Few dreamed that the larvae could tell them how long the body had been lying where it was found.

As one of their first projects, body farm researchers began watching the coming and going of insects throughout the decay process. It soon became clear that the tiny invaders fell into four groups, based on what they consumed. Necrophagous types fed on decaying flesh and included flies and some types of beetles. Predatory types—usually beetles—fed on flies, their eggs, and their larvae. A mixed group such as ants and wasps fed on both the corpse and on other predatory species, and the herbivorous group fed on decaying vegetation and fungi in the soil under the corpse. Researchers also noted that there was a pattern of

arrival of insects, which they called faunal (animal) succession. The pattern of succession was predictable, although there were variations in species depending on locale and time of year. Flies were the most reliable, always arriving within minutes of death and before other insects. They could also be counted on to quickly lay thousands of eggs that resembled piles of sawdust on the corpse. "[Flies] arrive on the scene before the police," says insect expert Bernard Greenberg. "They've got a very effective 911 number of their own."[42]

Shortly after flies deposited their eggs, a variety of beetles arrived. Some, such as rove beetles, hister beetles, and carrion beetles, invaded the corpse to feast on eggs and maggots. As the corpse dried, however, they moved away, and ham beetles and skin/hide beetles arrived to feed on the skin, exposed tendons, and bones. When nothing but bones were left, most of the insects left, too, but researchers found that tiny herbivorous soil beetles and springtails (six-legged, wingless insects) that had migrated to the soil under the corpse persisted for an indefinite period of time.

Within mere minutes of a person's death, flies begin to swarm around the corpse and then lay thousands of eggs, which hatch into maggots, pictured. Forensic entomologists can determine a lot about how long a person has been dead based on the size and age of maggots.

Becoming a Forensic Entomologist

Job Description:

A forensic entomologist studies insects found at crime scenes in order to determine the postmortem interval, whether the body has been moved, and how the victim died. Work takes place both in the laboratory and in the field. In addition to aiding law enforcement officials, forensic entomologists often teach and perform research at a college or university, act as consultants, and provide continuing education classes to law enforcement officials.

A forensic entomologist applies the knowledge of insects to the study of corpses in a criminal investigation.

Education:

Aspiring forensic entomologists must earn a bachelor of science (BS) degree in biology, zoology, or entomology, plus a master of science (MS) degree in entomology from an accredited college or university. Most forensic entomologists also earn a doctor of philosophy (PhD) degree in entomology and become certified by the American Board of Forensic Entomology.

Qualifications:

Aspiring forensic entomologists must be objective, persistent, and enjoy working with insects. They must be able to handle situations involving death and decay.

Salary:

$40,000 to $85,000 per year

What the Bugs Reveal

With new opportunities to study insects and human decomposition, numerous entomologists came to the Body Farm in Tennessee to carry out studies over the years. Their research projects were designed to be practical, and the results were quickly applied to crime solving. For instance, they were able to tell law enforcement that, when organisms like springtails and mites were found in soil, a body had once been at that locale, even if it was no longer there. If a body showed unexpected areas of maggot infestation and advanced decomposition, they could know that the victim had sustained wounds in those areas because flies are drawn to blood. If a blood-sucking insect such as a louse was found on a victim, that insect could be analyzed to see if it contained a perpetrator's DNA (genetic material unique to each human being) and perhaps identify him.

The most significant research yielded the breakthrough discovery that insects could be used to help determine time since death. Calculations were usually based on fly life cycles: The flies arrive and lay eggs on a body, the eggs hatch, and larvae grow and shed their hard exoskeletons according to very predictable timetables. For instance, at a temperature of 80.6°F (27°C), *Calliphora vicina* (bluebottle blowfly) eggs hatch twenty-four hours after being laid. First generation (instar) maggots eat and grow for twenty-four hours. They then molt (shed their skin) and enter the second instar stage which lasts twenty hours. Yet another molt puts them in the third instar stage, which lasts forty-eight hours, after which they go into the prepupa stage. Within the next 128 hours, they stop eating, move away from the body, form a hard protective shell, known as a puparium, and go into a resting stage. That final stage lasts for eleven days after which they hatch as adults.

By the Numbers

600

Number of species of insects that can visit a body from death through the skeletal stage

If blood–sucking lice are found on a victim, an analysis is done on the insects to see if they contain any DNA of the perpetrator.

The process of determining the postmortem interval (PMI) using flies first required identifying the species and age of the maggots on a body when it was found. Researchers then calculated backward to see when the eggs were laid. For instance, if *Calliphora vicina* maggots on a body were second instar size, crime scene investigators could know with certainty that they had been in that stage less than twenty hours, in first instar stage one day, and as eggs one day. That meant that they had been deposited on the body three days earlier, so it was likely that death had occurred about three days before.

Temperature and Decay

Whether insects or some other means was used to determine the PMI, everyone instinctively knew that temperature had to be taken into consideration because of its effect on decomposition. Food spoils more quickly in warm temperatures than in cold. There are more insects active on warm days than on cold ones. The exact correlation between temperature and decay was unknown, however, so researchers set out to learn more about it. For instance, they placed one body in the sun and a comparable one in the shade, and documented the differences in speed at which they broke down. They also noted previously uncharted variables, such as the fact that in sunny locales both the body and the ground absorbed and held heat. That warmth allowed bacteria and larvae activity to continue into the night when cooler air temperatures ought to have slowed activity down.

Other temperature-related factors such as seasons and climate had to be considered, too. Long, summer days produced conditions favorable to bacteria and insects and speeded up decomposition. When days shortened, decay slowed because of shorter periods of warmth. Cold-weather climates acted like freezers in the winter, preserving a body, preventing decay, and extending the decomposition period for months longer than expected.

Humidity was another important climate variable. When combined with warm temperatures, humidity increased the

Decomposition Variables

In a human body, the rate and manner of decomposition is affected by a number of factors. In roughly descending order, from most to least important, they include:

- temperature
- availability of oxygen
- embalming
- cause of death
- burial and depth of burial
- access by scavengers
- trauma, including wounds and crushing blows
- humidity or wetness
- rainfall
- body size and weight
- presence of clothing
- the surface on which the body rests

speed of decomposition dramatically. On humid summer days in Tennessee, for instance, bodies were found to completely decompose in as little as eighteen days. On the other hand, too much moisture, such as when a body was placed in water, slowed decomposition because tissues did not dry enough to attract insects that normally colonized the body during the late decay stages.

Temperature and Insects

Because temperature had such a significant impact on insect activity and decomposition, researchers found a way to mathematically factor it into their calculations when determining PMI. They developed the concept of accumulated degree hours

A fly feasts on a dead fish, as maggots crawl around nearby.

(ADH) and accumulated degree days (ADD), whereby insect development and decomposition rates could be standardized using the product of time and temperature. Bass and Jefferson explain: "Ten consecutive 70-degree days in summertime would total 700 ADDs (10 × 70); so would 20 wintertime days averaging 35 degrees apiece (20 × 35). In either season, winter or summer, a body at 700 accumulated degree days would exhibit similar signs of decomposition."[43]

To calculate ADH, researchers turned to tables published by entomologists like A.S. Kamal in the 1950s that give the developmental times for various fly species at controlled laboratory temperatures, usually 26.7°C (80°F). They then multiplied those times by the temperature. Blowfly maggots, for instance, take 34 hours to hatch and develop to the second instar in a 26.7°C lab. This means the total ADH for blowflies raised to second instar is 907.8 (34 × 26.7) or 37.8 ADD (907.8 divided by 24 hours in a day.) If the temperature was lowered to 25.5°C, the ADH to second instar was still 907.8 because the length of development time at the lower temperature was longer (about 35.6 hours).

Determining the PMI based on insect activity and using ADH or ADD was somewhat complicated but effective. Researchers took maggots collected from the body and raised them to adults in a laboratory at a constant temperature. When they hatched, the ADH for the time they had been in the lab was noted, their species was identified from their appearance, and the total ADH for that species under laboratory conditions determined from tables. The ADH for the time in the lab was deducted from the total ADH; the remainder was the ADH the maggots were on the body before it was discovered. That remainder was divided by the average crime scene temperature to yield the number of hours the maggots were developing on the body at the crime scene. Counting back that number of hours from the time the body was discovered gives the approximate time that death occurred.

Environment's Role

As researchers grew to better understand the interplay of insects, temperature, and climate on decomposition, they realized that unique conditions in the environment immediately around the corpse could affect the process, too. For instance, a corpse lying in the desert might be expected to dehydrate and mummify at a certain rate, but if that corpse happened to be resting in the shade of a boulder in that desert, it would be in a slightly cooler environment and would perhaps dehydrate more slowly. A body lying in an airy, open living room of a house would quickly attract flies, but if it was shut in a closet in that living room, it would not.

To learn exactly how important a role the environment played, more studies were conducted, mimicking real-life victims and the types of conditions under which they died. Bass recalls, "[We] compared bodies on land to bodies submerged in water; the floaters lasted twice as long. [We] compared bodies on the surface to bodies buried in graves, ranging from shallow to deep; the deeply buried bodies took eight times as long to decompose as the exposed bodies."[44] Researchers compared overweight corpses to thin ones; surprisingly the overweight ones skeletonized faster because their flesh fed a larger number of maggots. Corpses that were hung decayed less quickly than ones on the ground because feeding maggots fell off and were not able to get back on the body to consume it. Burned corpses decayed faster than unburned ones because small cracks in the skin allowed insects to penetrate the flesh more easily.

Bodies were studied clothed and naked; those that were naked generally decomposed faster because insects could get to body openings faster. Researchers had to add at least two days to their estimates for decomposition if a body was wrapped in a tarp because flies could not access it as quickly as if it were uncovered.

Down to the Bone

No matter how many studies were conducted, there were always new questions that needed to be answered. Many came from cases that law enforcement encountered in the field. No one understood, for instance, why the upper part of a corpse, lying clothed on the ground, would reduce to bones while the lower part retained its flesh. Or why the uppermost victim in a double grave decayed while the corpse underneath showed little sign of decomposition.

Many of the questions involved bones. Bass himself had always been particularly fascinated by bones. They were his specialty, and he knew that they could provide an abundance of information about how a person died. Thus, from the beginning, they were an important part of body farm research. He and Jefferson point out that "flesh forgets and forgives ancient injuries; bone heals, but it always remembers: a childhood fall, a barroom brawl, the smash of a pistol butt to the temple, the quick sting of a blade between the ribs. The bones capture such moments, preserve a record of them, and reveal them to anyone with eyes trained to see the rich visual record."[45]

CHAPTER 4

Secrets in the Bones

Because bones are a rich source of information for forensic experts, a significant amount of work done at body farms involves studying the skeletons of the men and women who decay there. Not only do skeletons give indications of trauma that occurs during a crime and over the course of a lifetime, but they can also be compared to skeletons from earlier eras, so that changes in height, weight, and shape can be documented. Forensic anthropologist William M. Bass states, "The human skeleton is changing surprisingly quickly ... so it's important for anthropologists to track that sort of skeletal changes. [And] when the bones of an unknown murder victim are found, their measurements can be compared to all the data from our collection to help pin down the age, race, and sex of that victim."[46]

Collecting and Cleaning

Staff and students have to be thoroughly familiar with bones before carrying out research. They learn early on that the adult human skeleton contains 206 bones, which are divided into four classes—long, short, flat, and irregular. They become so familiar with each that they can identify even a small piece of a finger bone, for example, without difficulty. They know exactly how a skeleton falls apart as it decays and the ligaments, tendons, cartilage, and muscles disappear. Forensic anthropologist and former Body Farm student Emily Craig says, "When a corpse is laid out on the ground, gravity sucks the bones downward so that the skeleton eventually collapses, settling into earth made soft and soggy from the decaying tissues. What once was a rib cage becomes a flat row of rib bones, while the spine turns into a collection of disarticulated [disconnected] vertebrae."[47]

It is the task of graduate students at body farms to collect a subject's bones after a decomposition project is complete. Putting on gloves and glasses to protect themselves from disease-causing bacteria, they pick up each piece, check its name off a list, and carefully place it in a collection bag. Trowels and a metal screen are used at the end of collection so that even tiny finger and toe bones hidden in dirt and debris can be recovered.

Bone analysis is an important part of forensic investigation. Here, a fine brush is used to carefully remove dirt from around a bone so that is can be collected and studied.

Once the bones are retrieved, they are taken to the indoor lab where the cleaning process begins. Again wearing safety glasses and gloves, researchers put the bones in large stainless steel kettles that are filled with water, detergent, and bleach. "Sometimes we have to cut them apart to fit,"[48] explains Texas State anthropology professor Michelle Hamilton, who was a graduate assistant at the University of Tennessee before moving to Texas State.

Electric crock pots are set up to hold smaller bones such as skulls, hands, and feet. Everything is simmered on low heat, filling the air with the smell of decay and cooked meat, until

Cleaning Bones

Bones must be cleaned before they can be studied, and rough or careless processing can damage them. The following steps are generally followed:

1. Using dissecting tools, including a scalpel, tweezers, and forceps, remove skin and large bundles of tendons, muscles, and ligaments.

2. Place bones in a metal kettle and cover with a bleach and water solution. Small or fragile bones can be placed in a crock pot or a metal strainer within the kettle to protect them from damage.

3. Bring water to a boil, then reduce heat to a simmer.

4. Simmer bones until remaining attached tissue softens and loosens. Bones should not be left in bleach too long as it can etch and destroy their surface.

5. Remove bones from solution and rinse thoroughly. Gently scrape or brush to remove additional tissue.

6. Repeat simmer step using detergent instead of bleach as needed until all tissue is removed.

Remove bones from kettle, place on towel, and allow to dry.

most of the flesh falls off. The bones are then removed from the pots, cleaned with scissors, tweezers, and toothbrushes, and laid out to dry. After examination, they are coated with a preservative and placed in specially designed boxes. The boxes are labeled with the age, sex, and race of the subject, and then shelved on tall metal racks in storage rooms. Journalist Terry Moseley writes, "Regardless of the size of the adult body in life, almost every skeleton can be neatly tucked into a box measuring 3 feet by 1 foot by 1 foot."[49]

Reading the Bones

Examination of the bones after they are cleaned yields vital information needed to solve crimes. Identity can be determined by matching teeth found in a skull to a missing person's dental records. If no dental records are available, teeth can still be useful to determine the age of the victim so police can narrow their search. If permanent teeth have not erupted, for instance, investigators know they are looking for a child younger than five years old. If all permanent teeth have erupted, the victim is at least seventeen years old. Worn or missing teeth can indicate an older victim.

The state of other bones can also help determine an unidentified victim's age. Microscopic examination of thin slices of long bones can reveal the condition of osteons—structural units—which fragment as a person ages. The disappearance of cartilage at the end of long bones and between other bones is another sign of maturity. Porous, ragged, and sharp edges on ribs and pelvic bones are sure signs of approaching old age.

The gender or sex of the victim can also be determined from the bones. Male bones are normally larger than female bones, and bony knobs where muscles attach are heavier on males because men have larger muscles than women. Male

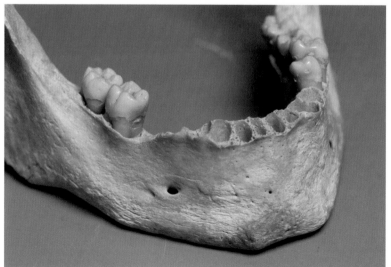

A person's identity can often be made by matching teeth in a skull to a missing person's dental records.

A corpse's bones last the longest, but hair is made up of dead cells, so it does not decompose as fast as soft tissues do.

skulls are conspicuous for their heavy brow ridges and they have a large knob—the external occipital condyle—at the base where several neck muscles attach. On the other hand, the female pelvic inlet (the space in the center of the pelvic girdle) is larger than a male's because a baby must be able to pass through during the birthing process.

Usually bones can indicate ethnicity. In general, skull bones of individuals of African (or Negroid) descent are heavier and smoother than those of Asians, Native Americans, and Caucasians. Eye sockets are more rectangular, nasal openings are broader, and a trait known as prognathism—in which the teeth and lower jaw jut forward—is apparent in African skulls. Skulls of persons of Caucasian descent (Caucasoid) are noticeably long and thin, while those of Asian descent (Mongoloid) are rounder than other racial groups. In Asian groups as well, eye sockets are round, cheekbones are flat, and front teeth show ridging on the inside edges that can be distinctive. In the future as more people of mixed race are born, these traits will become

The Bones Last Longest

Whenever a badly decayed corpse is found, crime scene investigators do their best to create a biological profile to help identify the victim. In the following excerpt from her book, Teasing Secrets from the Dead, *forensic anthropologist Emily Craig explains how bones and other evidence are important aids in creating that profile:*

Every biological profile ... would ideally include the anthropologist's "Big Four": sex, age, race, and stature. If you're lucky, and you've got the evidence to go further, you can put in ancillary [secondary] information such as weight and maybe hair color. Often, human remains do survive with enough intact hair to determine color, because hair is made up of dead cells, which don't decompose as soft tissues do. Even a single long, blond hair found stuck to the underside of a skull can help tremendously when you are trying to identify skeletal remains.

Sometimes the associated evidence—evidence found with a body or remains—can give you a clue. Clothing, for example, can help you determine a person's weight and size, though, of course, it too tends to decompose. In the end, though, the bones last longest—and they hold many secrets if you know what to look for.

Emily Craig, *Teasing Secrets from the Dead: My Investigations at America's Most Infamous Crime Scenes.* New York: Crown, 2004, p. 55.

less distinctive and it will be harder to determine ethnicity. As Bass and journalist Jon Jefferson observe, "eventually the human races will tend toward one human race, with a common, shared set of skeletal characteristics. In the meantime ... it's helpful to be able to tell police whether an unknown murder victim is white, black, Asian, or Native American."[50]

New Discoveries

Because bones are constantly being studied, new information and new means of identifying unknown victims are discovered regularly. For instance, in the early 1990s, Emily Craig entered Bass's PhD program and attended his human identification class. As usual, during the first semester, Bass asked the class to identify the ethnicity of a skeleton. The request was a trick. The bones had come from a black man, but the skull had no Negroid characteristics. Its bones were not heavy, and the teeth and jaws did not exhibit prognathism. No one had ever identified the skeleton correctly. Even Bass had mistakenly identified it as Caucasian until X-rays of a known missing person proved him wrong.

Bass expected everyone in the class to misidentify the skeleton, so he was surprised when Craig correctly stated that the victim had been black. Thinking that she had cheated and gotten the information from a former student, Bass confronted her. "How did you know? Everybody gets that wrong. They take a look at that skull and they're sure it's Caucasoid."[51]

Craig explained that she had not based her answer on the shape of the skull. She had looked at the knee. During the course of her former career as a medical illustrator, she had looked at thousands of knee joints, and she had observed that the angle of the intercondylar notch (a small groove at the end of the thigh bone) was different in Caucasians than in blacks. Bass was fascinated and encouraged Craig to do further research on knees. As a result, she devised a formula that allows law enforcement to differentiate Negroid and Caucasian femurs with 90 percent accuracy.

Broken Bones

In addition to finding new ways to identify unknown victims, body farm researchers study bones to better translate acts of violence into evidence. First they note the variations in shape and thickness that result from bones being broken and healed. They learn to recognize the difference between bones that were

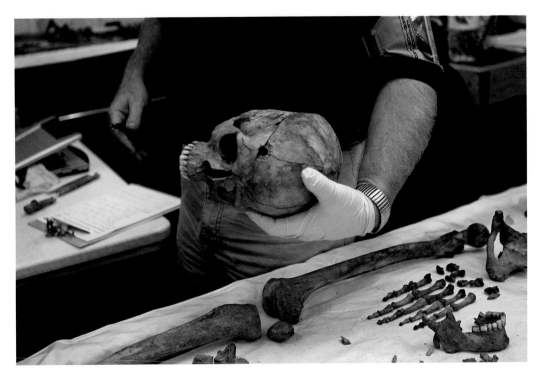

injured when the victim was alive, those that were injured at the time of death, and those that were injured long after death. Craig says, "The nature of bone changes ... radically after the body dies. When a person is alive or very recently dead, his or her bones resemble green wood. If you stick a knife into what we call a 'green bone,' you can pry up a little sliver, because the bone—living tissue—is still pliable. If you try to make the same cut days or weeks after death, the bone is more like firewood—dead and dried-out wood."[52]

A forensic expert holds a human skull that shows a bullet hole. Analysts who study bullet trajectory can recognize important patterns.

Researchers not only learn to recognize signs of past abuse in bones that have been injured and then healed, but they can also identify the crushing caused by hammers and tire irons, as well as the nicks, punctures, and slices caused by sharp objects such as knives, axes, and scissors. They recognize the pattern of fractures that are a result of a body being struck or run over by a car. They know that bullet holes in skulls leave distinctive entry and exit marks, and that bullets striking bones can chip or shatter them, depending on the angle of impact. Researcher Corey Sparks made a special study of the trajectory (curved path) of bullets as they entered and left a skull using digital scans and a computer. In the course of his project, he worked on a murder case in which a man claimed to have accidentally killed his wife while cleaning his rifle. Sparks explains, "We scanned her skull … and we found that the bullet had to have come from directly above her. So we proved it was murder."[53]

Beginning in the 1980s, researcher Steven Symes made sharp force trauma—specifically saw and knife marks—his area of expertise. After police discovered several dismembered victims and Symes could not tell them what kind of saw had been used to cut up the bodies, he purchased every type he could find, from jeweler's trim saws to lumberjack chain saws. Then, with a collection of bones and a bench vise, he made thousands of cuts, each of which he studied under a microscope. He also took measurements, made plaster impressions, and photographed the marks, while cataloging the characteristics of push strokes, pull strokes, false starts, skips, and hesitations. After years of research, he is now able to identify with certainty what kind of saw was used to dismember a victim, as well as the width and spacing of the saw teeth.

Burned Bones

Another type of trauma that body farm researchers study is the effect of fire on bone. They set up burn sites and incinerate parts of human bodies under various conditions, retrieve and examine the bones afterward, and carefully document their findings. Some of what they have already learned includes the fact that skulls split apart into small pieces in a fire; and that bones blacken, become gray, and then carbonize to white as all the organic material burns away. The mineral

components that are left are called "calcined" bone and are fragile to the touch.

Earlier researchers believed that fire destroyed all traces of a crime, but at the Body Farm, researchers learned to reassemble bones after a fire, so that identity could be established and trauma plainly seen. Bass used this knowledge to help solve a case that was puzzling police in 1989. Bone fragments were all that was left of a middle-aged male who had died in a car fire early that year. The man was believed to be Owen Rutherford, who had had financial difficulties and had last been seen a few months before. The body in the car had been burned beyond recognition, and because Rutherford's life had been insured for $250,000, insurance investigators wanted to be sure that he had not faked his death in order to get the money.

After examining the car and the totally burned remains, Bass determined that the fire had been exceptionally hot. It took a great deal of heat to burn a body which is 65 percent water. In this case, not only had the flesh almost completely

A blackened skull lies in a mass grave in Haiti. Body farm researchers study the effects of fire on bones.

When there are no other means of identifying skeletal remains, such as when a body is badly burned, forensic scientists can rebuild skulls from bone fragments found at the crime scene to help provide a likeness of the victim.

burned away, but the bones that remained had also split apart. Bass wondered if an accelerant such as gasoline had been used in an attempt to destroy all traces of a murder.

Collecting the bone fragments, he took them back to his lab where he painstakingly pieced them together. Rutherford's doctor had provided X-rays taken in life, and Bass looked for some unique form or structure in the bones that he could match to the X-rays. Finally, he was successful. X-raying the recreated frontal bone of the skull, he saw that the edges of the sinuses were scalloped, with a wavy line of bone running vertically to separate them. Rutherford's X-rays showed an identical pattern. There were two impacted wisdom teeth in the jawbone of the unidentified skeleton, and these were clearly present in Rutherford's X-rays, too. Bass could not tell if the case was a murder or not, but he got satisfaction from making the identification.

The Fighter's Position

While studying burned bodies, body farm researchers found that fire caused muscles to contract in predictable ways, leaving clear evidence for investigators to find. In the following excerpt from the article "Burning Evidence: Burning a Body Can't Cover Up Everything," forensic expert Doug Hanson explains:

In the case of arson fire or of a faked car accident and fire, the body is generally badly decomposed, but the skeletal structure remains largely intact. If a person is alive but unconscious before they are burned, the burned body will assume a pugilistic [fighter's] posture. This term arises from the similarity of the posture to that of a boxer in the ring; the arms are raised up in a defensive position and the hands are tightened into fists. The legs may be bent into a defensive stance as well. As a body burns, the muscles contract and the flexor muscles, being stronger, overpower the extensor muscles, thus giving rise to the pugilistic position of the body. If a burned body is found with one or both hands with the fingers extended and not in the pugilistic position (as a fist), this would indicate that one or more of the three bones of the arm had suffered a fracture before the victim died. This fracture would most likely have occurred from some form of blunt force trauma or from a beating.

Doug Hanson, "Burning Evidence: Burning a Body Can't Cover Up Everything," Officer. com, November 22, 2006, www.officer.com/web/online/Investigation/Burning-Evidence/18$33683.

The Bone Collectors

Whether bones are whole, broken, or burned, body farm administrators are careful to preserve them for future generations to study. Over the years, the Forensic Anthropology Center in Tennessee has come to house the world's largest collection of modern skeletons. The collection includes the William M. Bass Forensic Skeletal Collection, which consists of over three hundred complete and partial skeletons, some of them unidentified, predominantly from Tennessee. There is also the William M. Bass Donated Skeletal Collection, which contains complete skeletons of more than four hundred identified individuals. Each has been carefully measured as well as scanned using computerized axial tomography, creating three-dimensional images. The collection is unique because of the diversity of its subjects. Early collections usually contain older Caucasians, but the Bass collection includes Caucasians, Africans, and Hispanics ranging from prebirth to over one hundred years old. The collection is also unique because it illustrates how bones change as a result of societal changes, such as better eating habits, less hard labor, and improved medical care. Director Richard Jantz points out, "We're taller than we were more than 100 years ago. The shape of the skull is higher, narrower, and longer. The teeth and jaws, like the rest of the skeleton, are experiencing less stress, so they are becoming smaller."[54]

As technology improved over the years, Jantz organized what had been learned about the skeletal collections into a forensic data bank. The data bank contains detailed skeletal information from individuals worldwide and helps forensic scientists more easily determine the race and ethnicity of unknown remains. Dozens of groups from Europeans to Australian Aborigines are included in the files.

In the 1990s using data-bank information, Jantz and computer expert Stephen Ousley created software named FORDISC (forensic discriminant function analysis), designed to aid others in identifying skeletal remains. FORDISC is based on measurements of thousands of bones and is continually being updated with data from body farm researchers and other forensic anthropologists. When a set of remains needs to be identified, bone measurements are entered into the computer, the numbers are compared with the database, and a classification of racial or ethnic origin is given. The program is used by international tribunals investigating war crimes, in human rights investigations, and by law enforcement, seeking to identify a victim. In one 1991 case, for instance, police had unsuccessfully searched records of missing Caucasian males in order to identify a set of remains. After measurements of the remains were entered into FORDISC, it indicated that the victim was black, and he was then was quickly identified. Bass and Jefferson write, "In several … US murder cases … ForDisc has played a pivotal role in focusing or refocusing efforts to identify unknown victims."[55]

Respect for the Dead

Skeletal collections are only in the early stages of creation at the North Carolina and Texas body farms, but like in Tennessee, researchers always keep in mind that the bones they work with were once living, breathing human beings. If family members want to come and visit their loved ones, then they are welcomed, conducted to a private room, and given time alone with the boxed remains as if they were visiting a grave.

In Tennessee researchers even conduct an annual memorial service. Bass explains, "We just go in and randomly pick a box from the other room and take it over to one of the little classrooms, and we have a chaplain from the hospital who comes over and does a religious service for all the individuals. We invite the students that work here and give notice to the people in town who have donated their loved ones. Sometimes they come, sometimes they don't."[56]

As researchers show respect for the dead and honor those

who decide to leave their bodies to the facility, they sometimes think about their own deaths, and whether they will become a body farm resident. Surprisingly, many experience misgivings about making the facility their final resting place. Perhaps it is the fact that it is their workplace, and they cannot picture themselves resting there. Perhaps they are uncomfortable with the idea of fellow researchers watching them decompose. For whatever reason, even Bass has not made up his mind. He says, "I'll leave that call to [my wife] Carol and the boys [sons Charlie, Billy, and Jim]. The scientist in me wants to sign the donation papers. But the rest of me can't forget how much I hate flies."[57]

CHAPTER 5

Soil and Scent

As many of the questions regarding bodies, decay, and time of death were answered over the years, research at body farms expanded to take in the more subtle aspects of the decomposition process. Specifically, researchers are now investigating the byproducts of decomposition found in soil, molecular changes in decomposed tissue, and decompositional odors as means of locating a corpse and/or pinpointing time of death. "Hi-tech is where it's going," says Richard Jantz, director of the Forensic Anthropology Center in Tennessee. "I can see us doing a lot more biochemical work. I can see us doing more DNA work and DNA degradation."[58]

Byproducts in Soil

One researcher who focuses on decay at the molecular level is Arpad A. Vass, who began working at the Body Farm in the late 1980s and has since taken a position in the Life Sciences Division of Oak Ridge National Laboratory (ORNL), about 25 miles (40km) from Knoxville. He remains a regular visitor to the Body Farm, as well as an associate professor of forensic anthropology at the University of Tennessee's Law Enforcement Innovation Center in Knoxville.

Vass initially believed he could come up with a new method of determining time of death through bacterial analysis. He hoped to prove that bacteria developed on a dead body in succession patterns similar to those of insects. When he attempted to carry out his experiments, however, he realized that the idea was impractical. The corpse he laid out was immediately flooded by multitudes of species of bacteria, so that it was impossible to document and keep track of them. He writes, "I came to the conclusion … that with the exception of micro-organisms living in deep sea vents, every micro-organism known is involved in some aspect of the human decompositional cycle."[59]

Abandoning his bacterial focus, Vass looked for another possible means of determining time since death. No one had studied the fluids that ooze out of a corpse, so he began researching those, taking samples of soil from under the body and doing a molecular analysis of the decay byproducts found in it. He discovered that those byproducts contain a mixture of fatty acids—carbon-based molecules found throughout the body—released when organs and tissues decay. Studying them, Vass noted that the ratio of the fatty acids to one another changed as the body decomposed. For instance, at three hundred accumulated degree days, there was more than twice as much propionic acid as isovaleric acid. At nine hundred accumulated degree days, there was twice as much isovaleric acid as propionic.

Byproducts Timeline

Using seven subjects (two black males, a white female, and four white males) who were laid out in the Body Farm at various times of the year and allowed to decompose, Vass collected his soil byproduct data every three days in the spring and summer, and weekly in the fall and winter. After months of work, he was able to prove that, although the ratios of fatty acids change over time, they are essentially the same for every body at comparable points in the decomposition process. In fact, they create a byproduct timeline that he believed could be used to determine how long a body had been decomposing and leaching fluids into the soil. All he had to do was document the ratios, and they could then be compared to ratios from soil under a corpse at a crime scene.

After refining his process, Vass was able to estimate time since death with an accuracy of plus or minus two days for every month of decay. Bass and journalist Jon Jefferson write, "Arpad [Vass] can correlate chemistry with time, and read the decay products like a clock that has been ticking off the hours or days or weeks since death."[60] The technique proved workable even if

body fluids are recovered from mattresses, carpeting, clothing, and the like. And, as a secondary finding, Vass discovered that body fluids can be used to help determine ethnicity of a badly decomposed corpse. Melanin—the pigment that gives skin its dark color—is another recoverable compound that leaches from the body during decay. Analysis of byproducts of black subjects yields high concentrations of melanin. Caucasian subjects have dramatically lower concentrations.

Experts can study soil and the body fluids found in the soil to help determine how long a corpse has been decomposing.

Vass's byproduct timeline works as long as the body releases moisture. After a few weeks, however, no soft tissue remains, and the source of fatty acids dries up. At that point, ratios level off and examiners cannot determine how much time has passed between drying and discovery of the body. Vass therefore continues to look at other time-dependent biological markers (biomarkers) that might give him a longer timeline. Skeletal byproducts—specifically inorganic compounds, including sodium, potassium, and calcium that are released from the bones as they slowly decompose—appear promising. Like tissue, bones have characteristic breakdown patterns and consistent ratios of

Identifying Unknowns

Gas chromatography/mass spectrometry has been widely acclaimed in forensic science because it can positively identify the presence of a particular element in a given sample. The gas chromatograph heats a liquid sample of an unknown substance until it is vaporized into a gas, then funnels the vapor through a coil-shaped structure lined with chemicals. The various elements in the gas travel at different speeds through the structure, with small molecules traveling faster than larger ones. A detector monitors the molecules as they emerge from the structure, with smaller molecules exiting sooner than larger ones. Elements are identified electronically by the order in which they emerge and by the retention time of the unknown substance in the column.

After passing through the gas chromatograph, the newly separated elements are run through a mass spectrometer, where molecules are separated according to their different masses (comparable to their weight), then counted. Their numbers are then sent to a computer, where a graph of the number of particles with different masses is created. This is known as the mass spectrum of the unknown and is unique from every other element.

inorganics that are released over time. Unlike tissue, however, the inorganics leach from the skeleton for years. Using them, Vass has been able to create postmortem interval (PMI) estimates that are accurate to within three weeks per year for up to five years.

Molecular Decomposition

Vass's projects were the first of many that focused on decomposition on a molecular level. Another that has shown promise involves identifying biomarkers—substances that can be used as indicators—in human tissue, rather than in soil and other materials. Researchers hope that if biomarkers can be used to

create a decomposition timeline, they will be able to accurately pinpoint time since death even before the body begins releasing byproducts.

In the first study researching tissue biomarkers at the Body Farm, samples of various organs and muscles were collected from eighteen subjects at hourly intervals as bodies decayed. Collection took place for about three weeks, with researchers sampling heart, kidneys, brain, and muscles to determine if there was one organ that provided the best indicator of time since death. The samples were run through two machines—a gas chromatograph and a mass spectrometer—which separated and identified the components of each sample. Researchers then looked to see if there was a constant rate at which some compounds broke down. If there was, they hoped to be able to link specific amounts of it to specific stages of decomposition as they had with other compounds.

Body farm researchers have studied many organs, including kidneys, pictured, to determine whether one provides the best indicator of time since death.

Distinct patterns were indeed revealed that looked useful for determining the PMI. Currently, the compound oxalic acid and its derivative, glycolic acid, show the most promise in making determinations. Their levels are not dependant on the size or weight of the subject, and they are found in a variety of organs. Thus, if the liver is damaged by trauma, researchers can still take tissue from the heart, kidneys, brain, or muscles and

Future PMI Tests

Scientists throughout the world continue to search for more accurate ways to determine of time of death. In the following excerpt from Corpse: Nature, Forensics, and the Struggle to Pinpoint Time of Death, *author Jessica Snyder Sachs explains one technique that shows potential:*

[Researchers] are pioneering entirely new tests for postmortem interval based on such things as the breakdown of nuclear and mitochondrial DNA.... Among the most promising is a test of bioelectrical impedence [resistance] across various parts of a dead body. In essence, such a test measures the speed with which a small electric current passes through tissue.... What pathologists noticed was that in the first twelve to twenty-four hours after death, the natural impedence of any tissue gradually increases, for the simple reason that electricity passes more slowly through colder tissues. After twenty-four hours, impedence drops again as dying cells spill their electrolyte-rich fluid contents. By measuring this deceleration and subsequent acceleration of current through tissue, postmortem tests of impedence become a continuous measure of body cooling (algor mortis) followed by cell destruction (autolysis) that continues for up to seventy-two hours after death.

Jessica Snyder Sachs, *Corpse: Nature, Forensics, and the Struggle to Pinpoint Time of Death.* New York: MJF, 2001, pp. 257-58.

find oxalic acid. Studies continue, but researchers are hopeful that their work will translate into another definitive molecular method of determining the PMI in the near future.

Because of their keen sense of smell, cadaver dogs are frequently used to detect human remains.

Decompositional Odors

While experiments involving decomposition byproducts continue, researchers have also begun studying the molecular makeup of gases that are released during decomposition. To capture these gases for analysis, freshly dead corpses are buried in graves outfitted with a network of perforated pipes running below and above each body. The pipes open above ground and are fitted with absorbent carbon traps that collect odor molecules, generated as the body decomposes. When the contents of the traps are analyzed using gas chromatography and mass spectrometry, some 450 compounds can be identified. Thirty are consistently detectable in all soil types and at all burial depths. Researchers are working to assemble the compounds into a decompositional order

By the Numbers

450

Number of known odor compounds released by a body during decomposition

analysis computer database, which would be the first step in identifying an "odor signature" unique to human decomposition.

The research, which is ongoing, has more than one potential forensic application. Identified odor compounds might be used in the training of cadaver dogs—canines that detect buried or unburied human remains using their sense of smell. Currently, trainers use a variety of chemical substitutes that more or less accurately mimic the smell of death, or they carry a container of soil collected from under a corpse. The latter is putrid smelling and must be double wrapped to prevent it from saturating the air with its sickening odor. Trainers must also be extremely careful when working with this so-called dirty dirt so that they do not expose themselves to HIV/AIDS, hepatitis, and other diseases transmitted through body fluids.

Another possible application of odor analysis is the creation of a decomposition detector that is less expensive and more reliable than a dog's nose. The skills and abilities of cadaver dogs make them an esteemed part of forensic teams, but there are too few of them in the United States. "Five have been shown, to my knowledge, to be really good at it,"[61] says Vass. Their training is costly and time-consuming, and, like any living thing, they have their weaknesses. They must go out on search exercises regularly to maintain their skills. Even with the best of care, they suffer from colds and allergies that affect their sense of smell. They can also become tired, distracted, and/or discouraged during long-term recovery efforts.

With these problems in mind, researchers hope to one day perfect an electronic nose much like a metal detector that can be passed over the ground to pick up the odors of death. They also dream of creating an instrument that can scan a corpse, sense the current odor pattern and degree of tissue breakdown, and determine the PMI. "Although our ultimate goal would be to develop an odor-sensitive instrument that would tell us time since death, initially we're studying changes in odor pattern and intensity,"[62] explains former researcher Jennifer Love.

Radar and Corpses

At the same time that decompositional odor studies are being carried out, experiments that test ground-penetrating radar (GPR) are underway. The research is based on the fact that most murderers try to hide their victims in some way, usually by burying them. At times, a murderer is clever and organized enough to choose a site that can be covered with concrete afterward to make it extra secure. He pours a patio slab over the body in his backyard or he repaves the floor of his basement where he hid his victim.

Searching for such graves in the traditional way is extremely difficult for law enforcement. It takes time; involves costly heavy equipment, such as backhoes; and may never

Law enforcement officials use ground penetrating radar (GPR) devices to detect buried objects. Here, Chicago police and technicians use GPR in an attempt to find buried bodies at the home of the mother of serial killer John Wayne Gacy in November 2007.

uncover a body. Using the electro-magnetic wave pulses of GPR, on the other hand, requires less-expense and heavy labor. When the radar waves hit a buried object or a variation in the soil density, they reflect back to an antenna that picks up and records the variations. Law enforcement hope that they could use GPR to find clan-destine graves simply by passing a detector above the ground and watching for variations on a computer monitor.

Intepreting the variations is not easy, however. Sometimes, images that look like bodies are indeed bod-ies, as Love learned while working at a historic site in Pennsylvania. "Using ground-penetrating radar, we came across two buried bodies, who were apparently part of the Ephrata Cloister, a religious group,"[63] she remembers. At other times, the variations can be misleading. GPR seemed to indicate the presence of four bodies in the ground behind a Chicago apartment house where serial killer John Wayne Gacy's mother had lived in the 1970s. Gacy, who killed and buried twenty-seven young men under the floorboards of his home during that time, had been seen with a shovel outside of the building in the dead of night. His activity and the GPR images were suspicious, but when the site was finally excavated in 1998, nothing but a flattened sauce pan, a marble, wire, and roots were discovered.

Convinced that GPR images need further study before they can be a reliable forensic tool, researchers at the Body Farm have taken it on as a project. For an initial study, they buried several bodies at varied depths, then covered each with vari-ous thicknesses of concrete. Using GPR, they then scanned the sites and recorded and studied the various images they obtained. Again, the work is ongoing. "We'll also be testing the difference in results between industrial concrete versus what someone might use in their backyard,"[64] explains an unnamed participant.

Odor Chemistry

Scientists are only beginning to understand the molecular makeup of odors and how they are detected and perceived by humans. In an interview on the public radio program The Infinite Mind, *Columbia University biology professor Stuart Firestein gives further details:*

Odors are molecules with carbon "backbones" to which other molecules, like oxygen and hydrogen, adhere [bind]. When we sniff, we inhale odor molecules, which then bind to receptors in the nose. There are at least 3,000 molecules that we can distinguish and we have about 1,000 odor receptors in our noses. Different types of odor molecules activate different combinations of receptors, alerting us to what we are smelling... .

Scientists do not have a satisfactory way to classify smells scientifically. There's no olfactory [odor] equivalent to a color wheel. Smells are popularly classified according to their hedonic [pleasurable] qualities, in other words, "good" smells versus "bad" smells. Some odors, for instance sulphur-based compounds produced in rotting animals and vegetables, seem to be widely disliked but it's not known whether this dislike is hard-wired [instinctive] or learned. To a degree, perception of an unwholesome smell can be imaginary, as a professor of psychology famously proved when he introduced his students to a chemical that, while it couldn't be detected by some people, was found repulsive by those who could smell it. Explaining he was conducting an experiment in diffusion and olfaction, he opened a container of the chemical and set it on his desk. Soon students in the first and second rows began to wrinkle up their noses and gag. And, as you've probably already guessed, the substance was water.

Stuart Firestein, interview by Fred Goodwin, *The Infinite Mind*, LCMedia, April 30, 2003, www.lcmedia.com/mind268.htm.

Sniffing Out Murders

Research involving odor technology and GPR was put to a real-life test in February 2008, when a twenty-member team of investigators traveled to Nevada to search for possible victims of Charles Manson and his followers on the deserted Barker Ranch west of Death Valley National Park. The Manson "family" had used the ranch around the time of their murderous spree in Los Angeles in 1969 that took the lives of seven people, including actress Sharon Tate. One of the family members later stated that at least three people had been murdered and buried at Barker Ranch during that time as well.

The investigative team included Vass, as well as a cadaver dog who "alerted" to possible decomposition odors rising from a patch of ground. After the alert, Vass used an electronic sensor that strongly indicated that volatile organic compounds, given off by human bodies as they decay, lay under the soil. "It's a crude sniffer, [but] it gives us a quick indication of areas we want to come back to,"[65] he explained.

Marc Wise, left, and Arpad Vass use cutting-edge technology in February 2008 to measure the gas coming from the ground in an area in California where Charles Manson and his followers retreated to after a killing spree in 1969.

The investigators had planned to use a portable gas chromatograph/mass spectrometer to get more precise information about the odor compounds, but the machine was damaged on the trip to the ranch. They therefore took samples of the soil to be analyzed later, and then turned to GPR to look for bodies underground at the site. "We're getting the highest hits … where the ground is soft," stated ORNL scientist Marc Wise. "There's definitely something down there. We just can't know yet exactly what until we dig."[66]

"Still Developing the Science"

Despite all the high-tech signs that human bodies lay underground at Barker Ranch, when four exploratory holes were finally dug in May 2008, no human bones, bodies, or clothing were found. Researchers were left trying to figure out why dog and machines had so misled them. They finally concluded that native plants at the site produced many of the same chemical compounds they were testing for. In addition, the GPR had apparently bounced off roots and other natural features, such as anthills and magnetic rocks, beneath the surface. The failure was disappointing, but did not discourage Vass. He stated, "We're just not there yet. We did the best we could, but this was an exploratory excavation. We're still developing the science, still trying to understand how to work in an environment like this."[67]

The statement expresses body farm researchers' optimistic philosophy. Just as Bass was motivated by the Colonel Shy blunder, new generations push past setbacks to refine techniques, study variables, and identify new methods to help solve crimes. They study microbial DNA under corpses in hopes of finding another way to determine the PMI. They imagine fitting flies with microchip tracking devices and using them to find rubble-covered bodies after mass tragedies. They dream of bioengineered bacteria that might contain a fluorescent green protein that glows in the presence of decay compound. Sprayed on a suspected clandestine grave, the microbes could serve as tiny fluorescent detectors to confirm the presence of human remains.

Because of their creativeness, and because so much of their work has proven valuable in the field, body farm facilities have expanded from research centers to centers of information and education. A growing number of experts ranging from journalists to war crimes investigators take advantage of knowledge and opportunities found within the wooden privacy fences. "Everybody picks up the phone and calls us when they have questions about decomposing bodies," says researcher Joseph Hefner. "We hear from agencies all over the country."[68]

CHAPTER 6

Beyond Death's Acre

With worldwide recognition and the establishment of several new facilities across the United States, body farms have become more than macabre laboratories for studying the dead. They are producers of experts who go out of their gates to serve worldwide as crime scene specialists. They are schools for law enforcement officials who need to improve their skills. They are training grounds for medical teams who want hands-on experience working with human corpses. "I'm really surprised that so many people are interested in the Body Farm," forensic anthropologist William M. Bass stated in 2000. "This was set up because I needed to know what happened to bodies decaying in Tennessee. I never thought [it] would be famous."[69]

Valuable Assets

Community outreach was the first offshoot of basic research at the Body Farm in Tennessee. In his role as state forensic anthropologist, Bass regularly took students on field trips to crime scenes, so they could help law enforcement and get experience with real-life cases. In one of many such expeditions, they excavated the grave of a con man named Monty "Cadillac Joe" Hudson, who had been killed by a mobster named Fat Sam Passarrella. In another, they recovered and identified the remains of eleven workers blown to bits when an illegal fireworks factory exploded. Bass observes, "Many of my fellow forensic anthropologists—probably nine out of ten—have never worked a crime scene… . They stay clean and dry that way, but they also miss a lot of evidence that could reveal what happened to the murder victim."[70]

Several anthropologists who trained at the Tennessee body farm now work for the U.S. Army's Central Identification Laboratory. They help recover and identify the remains of soldiers who were prisoners of war or missing in action. Pallbearers pictured here carry the remains of an unidentified serviceman from the Vietnam War.

As more body farms are established, forensic response teams—students and faculty who are on call when law enforcement finds a skeleton or decomposing body—continue to be an important part of the research experience. In a February 2008 case in North Carolina, a team from the Forensic Osteology Research Station (FOREST) used their skills to retrieve human bones found in a remote area of Nantahala National Forest. The effort was complicated by the fact that hunters had used the spot to dump animal carcasses, so searchers needed to be able to distinguish human bones from animal remains. "They've always dropped whatever they were doing to help us in our investigations," says Brian Leopard of the Macon County, North Carolina, Sheriff's Department. "They help eliminate a lot of false leads. It is a valuable asset to the law enforcement community to have ... this expertise."[71]

As twenty-first century body farm researchers practice their skills, a host of earlier graduates apply what they learned to other careers. More than half of the forensic anthropologists in the United States today trained at the Tennessee facility. Eight of them work for the Army Central Identification Laboratory in

Hawaii, helping to recover and identify the remains of members of the U.S. military who were killed in action in past conflicts. Steven Symes works at the Mercyhurst Archaeological Institute in Erie, Pennsylvania; is on contract to provide tool-mark analysis to the Newark, New Jersey, Medical Examiner's Office; and lectures internationally on bone trauma. Douglas Owsley graduated with his PhD from the University of Tennessee (UT) in 1978 and is director of the Physical Anthropology Division at the Smithsonian Institute in Washington, D.C. He helped identify the remains of American journalists kidnapped in

Excavating a Grave

In order to collect and document every piece of evidence, crime scene investigators follow a set of steps when excavating a clandestine grave:

1 Photograph the gravesite before excavation and at each step thereafter.

2 Clear away debris and vegetation to expose disturbed ground.

3 Lay a grid around the perimeter of the grave using string or rope to aid in documenting evidence found in the grave.

4 Remove soil from the grave layer by layer. All soil should be sifted and checked for any evidence that may have been buried with the body.

5 When the body is reached, carefully remove soil from around it by hand or using small brushes and trowels.

6 Remove remains by hand and package for later identification and analysis.

After remains are removed, excavate and examine an additional 6 inches (15cm) of soil for further evidence such as teeth, small bones, and bullets.

Tennessee body farm alumnus William Rodriguez testifies at a trial. As chief deputy for special investigations for the U.S. Armed Forces Medical Examiner, he led the medical team that helped process mass graves in Kosovo in the late 1990s.

Guatemala in 1985 and the remains of U.S. soldiers from the Persian Gulf War. Jennifer Love, who received her PhD in physical anthropology in 2001, directs the Forensic Anthropology Department of the Harris County Medical Examiner's Office in Texas. In addition to identifying unknown victims, she also works on cold cases—past criminal cases that remain unsolved. She says, "I have case files that date back to 1957. In one case, we have three unidentified decedents who were teen boys, the victims of the [1973] mass murders by Dean Corll, David Owen Brooks and Elmer Wayne Henley."[72] Corll, Brooks, and Henley killed twenty-seven young men in the so-called Houston Mass Murders, the worst U.S. serial killing case up to that time.

Speaking for the Victims

While some body farm alumni help solve individual murders, others, like Murray Marks, use their skills to identify victims of mass tragedy and genocide. Marks has helped recover victims of political murders in South America, and states, "We're there to speak for the victims, for the people who don't have a voice. By doing that, we get ever closer … to making someone pay for the crime."[73] William Rodriguez, who earned a PhD from UT in 1984, went on to become chief deputy for special investigations with the U.S. armed forces medical examiner in

Washington, D.C. He led the U.S. medical team that helped process graves in Kosovo, a site of ethnic cleansing in the late 1990s. Although most of the remains he helped uncover were in an advanced state of decomposition, the bones provided hard evidence that victims had been shot, stabbed, beaten to death, and dumped in mass graves by Yugoslav and Serbian security forces.

Emily Craig was part of a team that identified bodies retrieved from the Branch Davidian compound in Waco, Texas. In April 1993, seventy-six members of the cult, led by self-appointed prophet David Koresh, died when the compound was stormed by FBI agents and burned to the ground. Craig helped piece together Koresh's skull after the fire and proved that he had not been killed by the FBI, but by a single gunshot, possibily self-inflicted. She writes, "No FBI agent could ever have gotten close enough to Koresh to press a gun to his skull—and [the] beveled hole ringed with soot could

Collecting Techniques

At the Body Farm in Tennessee, visiting law enforcement are taught techniques to collect trace evidence such as hair, fiber, glass, and dirt particles found at a crime scene. Those techniques include:

- picking: Clean forceps can be used to pick up evidence such as fingernails, cigarette butts, and single hairs.
- lifting: Tape or sticky paper can be firmly patted or rolled over small carpeted or upholstered areas to lift hairs or other particulate evidence.
- vacuuming: A vacuum cleaner equipped with a filter trap can be used to recover evidence from large areas of carpet or flooring.
- combing: A clean comb or brush can be used to recover trace evidence from the hair of an individual.
- clipping: Clean scissors or fingernail clippers can be used to recover debris from under fingernails.

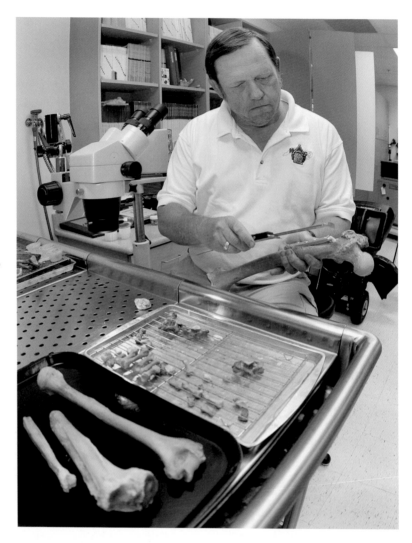

John Williams, director of the forensic anthropology program at Western Carolina University, examines part of a human femur bone from a cadaver. Williams is a member of a group of specialists on the Disaster Mortuary Operational Response Teams (DMORT), which deals with victim identification following mass fatality disasters.

only have been made by ... a contact gunshot wound to the forehead."[74]

Although not an alumni of the Body Farm, forensic anthropologist John Williams, head of FOREST, is a member of a team of specialists involved in Disaster Mortuary Operational Response Teams, part of the U.S. Department of Health and Human Services. The teams deal with victim identification and mortuary services after mass fatality disasters. Shortly after the terrorist attacks on September 11, 2001, in the United States, Williams spent about two weeks sorting through debris from

Ground Zero—site of the destroyed twin towers of the World Trade Center in New York. A founding member of the U.S. Department of Homeland Security, Williams also has assisted in the identification of victims of at least two airline crashes.

Training Centers

Body farms are not only launching pads for highly skilled and motivated forensic experts, but they have also become hands-on classrooms for individuals other than anthropology students. A variety of men and women involved in forensic fields, including medical examiners, police officers, private investigators, forensic dentists, and archaeologists visit the facilities, where classes are held on topics ranging from locating clandestine graves to evidence recovery. Some individuals come from as far away as Europe and Asia to pursue studies that are not available elsewhere. For instance, British expert Andrew Hart of the Forensic Science Service, the leading provider of forensic science services to the police forces of England and Wales, traveled to Tennessee in 2005 and 2006 to study insect

Law enforcement officers watch as a car burns during a training session for the National Forensics Academy in Knoxville, Tennessee. The academy is part of the University of Tennessee and considered to be one of the most comprehensive of its kind.

activity on dead bodies. "My research in entomology will add another powerful investigative tool to the fight against crime,"[75] he stated.

Some experts visit body farms to learn the fine points of evidence collection and preservation—how to choose a representative sample of insects from a crime scene, for instance, or how to examine and collect soil from under and around a corpse. FBI teams visit the Tennessee facility regularly to sharpen their bone-identifying and corpse-collecting skills. DMORT members, training to respond to weapons of mass destruction, come to develop methods for cleansing human remains of biological or chemical contaminants. "Our job is to go in and attempt to decontaminate human remains so they can be handled through other regular channels," says Steve Tinder, a member of the team. "This is the first exercise of this type ever, but I can guarantee you it won't be the last. We're all here to learn because there are no experts in this field—yet."[76]

Among the most regular visitors to the Body Farm in Tennessee are attendees of the National Forensic Academy, located at Oak Ridge National Laboratory. The one-of-a-kind institute offers a ten-week training program, created in September 2001 and sponsored by the U.S. Department of Justice. It is designed to teach law enforcement personnel the best way to recover bodies and process crime scenes. Officers from at least forty-three states have attended, and agencies outside the United States want to send trainees as well. Those who are admitted must show an interest and aptitude for forensic work. They get four hundred hours of in-depth training in such varied skills as fingerprinting the dead and identifying burned remains. At the end of training, all undergo a full day of testing, which is administered by the FBI's Evidence Recovery Team. "This is the only operation of its kind in the world," said Jarrett Hallcox, program

National Forensic Academy

The National Forensic Academy (NFA), located at the Oak Ridge National Laboratory in Tennessee, was the inspiration of Phillip Keith, chief of the Knoxville Police Department in the year 2000. Like many Americans, Keith had followed the O.J. Simpson murder trial in 1995, and had been appalled by the mishandled evidence and the mistakes made at the crime scenes by law enforcement that had complicated legal proceedings. Keith approached University of Tennessee officials with a proposal for a training program that would better educate crime scene investigators and help standardize their procedures so that mistakes would be reduced.

The academy opened in 2001, offering three ten-week, intensive education sessions annually. Class size is limited to twenty students who are taught crime scene management methods, crime scene photography, and techniques for collecting evidence. They then undergo field training where they learn proper evidence collection and preservation in scenarios such as arson fires, vehicle explosions, and bombings. They document and analyze bloodstain evidence in mock crime scenes. They complete the course with a week at the Body Farm where they take part in bone scatter and body recovery exercises.

Students leave the course with valuable skills as well as relationships with other forensic experts with whom they can network in the future. NFA graduate Eric Rish of the Duluth, Minnesota, Police Department says, "[We] know that we will be able to work through most any situation. I also see us as a great resource for our department as well as the region."

Quoted in Phillip Jones, "The National Forensic Laboratory," *Forensic Magazine*, February–March 2007, www.forensicmag.com/articles.asp?pid=134.

manager of the academy. "We provide a soup to nuts [thorough] introduction to crime scene investigation. Our graduates have a practical base to build from, but they are not experts in any one discipline."[77]

Commissioned Studies

In addition to sharpening their skills, law enforcement and others sometimes turn to body farm staff to get answers to specific questions. For instance, the FBI asked the Tennessee facility to research how concealment in the hot trunk of a car affected the decomposition of hair. A group of attorneys suing a Georgia crematorium commissioned a study to find out what a wood-chipping machine does to bone. The Batesville Casket Company—the leading manufacturer of coffins in the world—requested a study to find out exactly what happens to bodies inside their containers.

Sometimes researchers are asked to set up an experiment to try to answer questions relating to a specific crime. "What we'll do is simulate that scenario … where something doesn't decompose the way it's expected to," says researcher Rebecca Wilson. "Is this natural, or is this because what the perpetrator did? But we will simulate [reproduce] a scenario like that and see if it is related to natural processes, or related to the incident."[78]

In a recent case, researchers were asked to use their cutting-edge research to help analyze newly discovered evidence. After two-year-old Caylee Anthony of Orlando, Florida, was reported missing in July 2008, samples from the trunk of her mother's car were sent to the Tennessee facility so that experts could carry out tests for decompositional odors. "[Dr. Arpad A. Vass] is doing the tests in his lab at ORNL [Oak Ridge National Laboratory], through his affiliation with the Forensic Anthropology Center,"[79] UT spokesman Jess Mayfield said.

In late August, Vass reported that he found chemical evidence of human decomposition in the car, leading investigators to believe that the child was dead. After further investigation, Casey Anthony, the child's mother, was arrested and charged with murder in July 2008. Caylee's remains were discovered near the Anthony family home in December 2008.

"The Ultimate Goal"

With law enforcement and the public more aware that body farms are invaluable assets to communities, supporters continue to hope that more such facilities will someday be established not only in the United States, but also in other parts of the world.

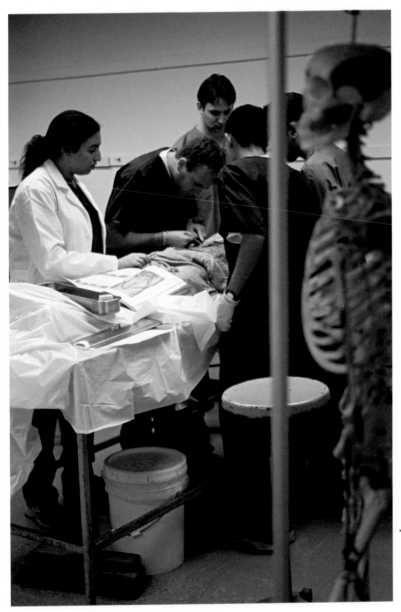

Forensic scientists believe there is much to be learned from studying human decay. Here, students study a cadaver in a laboratory.

Already in India, Roma Khan of the Investigative Scientific and Anthropological Analysis Facility is involved in planning one. She and her colleagues believe that there is still much more to be learned from studying human decay. Bass says, "I'd hope that we could get to the stage that after looking at everything in the body, we could tell you within a half-day how long that individual has been dead.... The ultimate goal [with bones] is to get enough data so you can look at any skeleton and make a 100-percent estimate of the age, sex, race and stature. I think it may come, that it is a possibility. It's a long way down the road, but that's what we're all looking for."[80]

Until that time, researchers tirelessly continue their work, knowing that they are helping decipher forensic mysteries, giving names to the nameless, and bringing murderers to justice. They may deal in death, but their work provides hope to many. Bass explains, "Our not-so-ivory-tower research, behind our locked gates and wooden fences, [equips] investigators with more and better tools to solve the crimes that occur in the real world. The world beyond the Body Farm."[81]

Notes

Introduction: "Ghastly Affront to Human Dignity"

1. Quoted in Jessica Snyder Sachs, *Corpse: Nature, Forensics, and the Struggle to Pinpoint Time of Death*. New York: MJF, 2001, p. 140.

2. Quoted in Bill Bass and Jon Jefferson, *Death's Acre: Inside the Legendary Forensic Lab the Body Farm Where the Dead Do Tell Tales*. New York: Berkeley, 2003, p. 119.

3. Quoted in Ken Beck, "Death Becomes Him," *Tennessean*, January 11, 2004.

4. Quoted in R.U. Steinberg, "Listening to the Bones," *Austin Chronicle*, April 4, 2008.

5. Bass and Jefferson, *Death's Acre*, p. 71.

Chapter 1: An Embarrassing Mistake

6. Bass and Jefferson, *Death's Acre*, pp. 62–63.

7. Bass and Jefferson, *Death's Acre*, p. 63.

8. Bass and Jefferson, *Death's Acre*, p. 67.

9. Quoted in John T. Dowd, "Colonel William M. Shy, Civil War Hero," *Tennessee Division, Sons of Confederate Veterans*, www.tennessee-scv.org/Camp854/shy2.html.

10. Bass and Jefferson, *Death's Acre*, p. 67.

11. Quoted in Sachs, *Corpse*, p. 64.

12. Bass and Jefferson, *Death's Acre*, pp. 94–95.

13. Bass and Jefferson, *Death's Acre*, p. 95.

14. Quoted in Katherine Ramsland, "The Body Farm," *truTV*, www.trutv.com/library/crime/criminal_mind/forensics/bill_bass/7.html.

15. Bass and Jefferson, *Death's Acre*, p. 96.

16. Bass and Jefferson, *Death's Acre*, p. 97.

17. Quoted in Chasing, "Interview: Body Farm and Buzzards," *Newsvine.com*, June 26, 2007, http://chasing.newvine.com/_news/2007/06/26/803033-interview-body-farms-and-buzzards.

18. Quoted in Greg Barrett, "UT Anthropologist Assumes Role of 'Caretaker' for Decaying Humans," *(Maryville, TN) Daily Times*, April 16, 2001.

19. Quoted in Lawrence Buser, "UT Professor Keeps an Eye on the Dead," *Commercial Appeal*, August 22, 1993.

Chapter 2: Death's Acres

20. Quoted in Kathleen Cullinan, "FGCU Wants to Become Leader in Studying Human Remains," *Naplesnews.com*,

April 4, 2007, http://m.naplesnews.com/news/2007/Apr/04/fgcu_wants_become_leader_studying_human_remains.

21. Quoted in Abigail Goldman, "Bone-Dry Dreams of a Body Farm," *Las Vegas Sun*, March 24, 2008, www.lasvegassun.com/news/2008/mar/24/bone-dry-dreams.

22. Quoted in Leonard Crist, "Plans for YSU Body Farm Bite the Dust," *Jambar*, April 13, 2006, http://media.www.thejambar.com/media/storage/paper324/news/2006/04/13/Pageone/Plans.For.Ysu.Body.Farm.Bite.The.Dust-1851464.shtml.

23. Susan Reinhardt, "Recent Government Letter Proved to Me That You Can Candy-Coat Dead Bodies," *Asheville (NC) Citizen-Times*, July 25, 2006.

24. Quoted in Emily Ramshaw, "Forensic Science—CSI-Style Unit Examines Bodies of Evidence—Neighbors May Object, but Research Helps Police Solve Cold Cases," *Dallas Morning News*, September 14, 2008.

25. Bass and Jefferson, *Death's Acre*, p. 94.

26. Quoted in Diane Martindale, "Bodies of Evidence," *New Scientist*, January 6, 2001, p. 24.

27. Terry Moseley, "(After) Life on the Farm—Former Dump Site Now a Laboratory of Human Flesh," *Chicago Tribune*, April 18, 2000.

28. Quoted in Rene Ebersole, "The Body Farm," *Current Science*, October 26, 2001, p. 10.

29. Bass and Jefferson, *Death's Acre*, p. 105.

30. Quoted in Wanda J. Demarzo, "Dead Body Farm Is a Lively Class for Cops," *Knight Ridder Newspapers*, February 18, 2004, www.fdiai.org/articles/dead_body_farm_is_a_lively_class.htm.

31. Quoted in Bryn Nelson, "Death Down to a Science/Experiments at 'Body Farm,'" *Newsday*, November 24, 2003.

32. Quoted in Gina Stafford, "UT Morgue Gets the Cure—Modern Pathology and Forensic Facilities Are Answer to Managed-Care Prayer," *Knoxville News Sentinel*, March 8, 1999.

33. Quoted in Todd Dvorak, "'Body Farm' Proposed to Study Rotting Corpses," *Live Science*, November 28, 2005, www.livescience.com/health/ap_051128_body_farm.html.

34. Quoted in Chasing, "Interview: Body Farm and Buzzards."

35. Quoted in Greg Barrett, "Strange Harvest at the Body Farm; Researchers Lift Clues of Death from a Field of Donated Cadavers," *USA Today*, April 16, 2001.

Chaper 3: Swarming with Insects

36. Quoted in Mike Osborne, "The Body Farm: Unique Forensic Research Facility," *Voice of America*, May 13, 2008, www.voanews.com/english/archive/2008-05/2008-05-13-voa39.cfm?CFID=22354461&CFTOKEN=72788193.

37. Quoted in Ramsland, "The Body Farm," *truTV*, www.trutv.com/library/crime/criminal_mind/forensics/bill_bass/4.html.

38. Emily Craig, *Teasing Secrets from the Dead: My Investigations at America's Most Infamous Crime Scenes*. New York: Crown, 2004, p. 50.

39. Bass and Jefferson, *Death's Acre*, p. 46.

40. Quoted in Claire Sibonney, "Corpse Doctor Provides Glimpse Inside the 'Body Farm,'" *Reuters*, December 22, 2007, www.reuters.com/article/lifestyleMolt/idUSN2121893120071222.

41. Bass and Jefferson, *Death's Acre*, p. 91.

42. Quoted in Frank James, "Don't Swat His Clues: The Sherlock Holmes of Entomology Uses Flies as His Assistants," *Chicago Tribune*, August 2, 1999.

43. Bass and Jefferson, *Death's Acre*, p. 241.

44. Bass and Jefferson, *Death's Acre*, p. 133.

45. Bass and Jefferson, *Death's Acre*, p. 34.

Chapter 4: Secrets in the Bones

46. Quoted in HarperCollins, "Author Interview: Dr. Bill Bass on *Beyond the Body Farm*," HarperCollins, www.harpercollins.com/author/authorExtra.aspx?authorID=32695&isbn13=9780060875299&displayType=bookinterview.

47. Craig, *Teasing Secrets from the Dead*, p. 44.

48. Quoted in Moseley, "(After) Life on the Farm."

49. Moseley, "(After) Life on the Farm."

50. Bill Bass and Jon Jefferson, *Beyond the Body Farm: A Legendary Bone Detective Explores Murders, Mysteries, and the Revolution in Forensic Science*. New York: HarperCollins, 2007, p. 137.

51. Bass and Jefferson, *Death's Acre*, p. 136.

52. Craig, *Teasing Secrets from the Dead*, p. 134.

53. Quoted in Lawrence Osborne, "Crime-Scene Forensics—Dead Men Talking," *New York Times Magazine*, December 3, 2000, p. 105.

54. Quoted in *Oak Ridge National Laboratory Review*, "Groundbreaking Science: Bone Diaries," *Oak Ridge National Laboratory Review*, www.ornl.gov/info/ornlreview/v37_1_04/article_19.shtml.

55. Bass and Jefferson, *Beyond the Body Farm*, p. 143.

56. Quoted in Ken Beck, "Death Becomes Him," *Tennessean*, January 11, 2004.

57. Bass and Jefferson, *Death's Acre*, p. 280.

Chapter 5: Soil and Scent

58. Quoted in Darren Dunlap, "The Plot Needs to Thicken," *Knoxville News Sentinel*, January 28, 2007.

59. Arpad A. Vass, "Beyond the Grave: Understanding Human Decomposition," *Microbiology Today*, November 2001, p. 192.

60. Bass and Jefferson, *Beyond the Body Farm*, p. xix.

61. Quoted in Nelson, "Death Down to a Science/Experiments at 'Body Farm.'"

62. Quoted in Oak Ridge National Laboratory, "ORNL Project Seeks to Pinpoint Time Since Death," news release, June 7, 2000, www.ornl.gov/info/press_releases/get_press_release.cfm?ReleaseNumber=mr20000607-00.

63. Quoted in Jo Ann Zuñiga, "Forensic Anthropologist Digs for Truth About Cases," *Texas Medical Center*, August 1, 2007, www.texmedctr.tmc.edu/root/en/TMCServices/News/2007/08-01/Forensic+Anthropologist.htm.

64. Quoted in Thecla Scully, "Body Farm for Human Decomposition Tests," *Irish Medical Times*, January 18, 2008, www.imt.ie/news/2008/01/body_farm_for_human_decomposit.html.

65. Quoted in Juliana Barbassa, "Forensic Testing Suggests Possible Manson Grave Sites," *Ventura County Star*, March 16, 2008.

66. Quoted in Barbassa, "Forensic Testing Suggests Possible Manson Grave Sites."

67. Quoted in Juliana Barbassa, "Questions Remain for Those Touched by Manson Murders," *Ventura County Star*, May 25, 2008.

68. Quoted in Adam Longo, "UT Forensic Anthropology Center Helps Law Enforcement Worldwide," *WATE.com*, April 26, 2006, www.wate.com/Global/story.asp?S=4822442.

Chaper 6: Beyond Death's Acre

69. Quoted in Moseley, "(After) Life on the Farm."

70. Bass and Jefferson, *Death's Acre*, p. 73.

71. Quoted in Western Carolina University, "Forensic Students Search for Clues in Murder," *newswise*, February 11, 2008, www.newswise.com/articles/view/537647.

72. Quoted in Zuñiga, "Forensic Anthropologist Digs for Truth About Cases."

73. Quoted in *Anatomy of a Corpse*, documentary, directed by Jon Jefferson, National Geographic Society, 2002.

74. Craig, *Teasing Secrets from the Dead*, p. 110.

75. Quoted in *Forensic Science Service*, "Return Visit to Body Farm for British Forensic Scientist and an Award from Her Majesty the Queen," *Forensic Science Service*, September 28, 2006, http://213.52.171.242/forensic_t/inside/news/list_press_release.php?case=58&y=2003.

76. Quoted in Don Jacobs, "Response Team Meets for Innovative Training—Body Farm Draws 'Family' of Experts Aiming to Hone Decontamination Methods," *Knoxville News Sentinel*, May 22, 2005.

77. Quoted in Anna C. Irwin, "TV Gives 'Bogus' Image of Crime Scene Investigators, NFA Manager Maintains," *(Maryville, TN) Daily Times*, November 26, 2006.

78. Quoted in Osborne, "The Body Farm: Unique Forensic Research Facility."

79. Quoted in Jim Balloch, "ORNL Scientist Aiding Missing-Toddler Case," *knoxnews.com*, August 15, 2008, www.knoxnews.com/news/2008/aug/15/ornl-scientist-aiding-missing-toddler-case.

80. Quoted in Randy Dotinga, "Professor Needs More Land for Bodies on Corpse Farm," *Wired.com*, December 12, 2007, www.wired.com/medtech/health/news/2007/12/body_farm.

81. Bass and Jefferson, *Beyond the Body Farm*, p. xxii.

Glossary

accumulated degree hours (ADH): The number of hours it takes for blowflies to develop multiplied by the temperature. By using the ADH and the temperature at a crime scene, investigators can calculate the approximate time of death.

algor mortis: The decline in body temperature in the hours after death.

anatomical order: The arrangement of bones or body parts to recreate the human body as it would lie with the feet together, the arms to the sides, and the head, eyes, and palms of the hands facing upward.

anthropology: The study of human beings.

autopsy: Examination of a corpse to determine cause of death.

biomarker: A substance, used as an indicator of a biological state or process, that can be objectively measured and evaluated.

byproduct: A secondary product obtained from a chemical reaction or a biological process.

DNA: An acronym for deoxyribonucleic acid, a genetic material unique to each individual that carries hereditary characteristics from adults to offspring.

entomology: The study of insects.

exoskeleton: A hard outer structure that provides protection or support for an organism, such as the shell of a snail.

FORDISC: Computer software designed to identify skeletal remains.

forensic anthropology: The study of bones and skeletons to determine gender, age, ethnicity, and cause of death in civil or criminal cases.

forensic entomology: The study of insects to aid in legal investigations.

herbivorous: Feeding on plants.

humidity: Moisture in the air.

inorganic: Compounds of mineral origin, such as sodium chloride, calcium carbonate, and calcium phosphate.

instar: A period of growth between molting in insects.

livor mortis: Discoloring of parts of the body due to settling of blood after death.

molt: To shed an outer skin or covering.

necrophageous: Feeding on carrion or corpses.

nocturnal: Active at night.

osteology: The study of bone function and structure.

osteon: The fundamental structural unit of compact bone, consisting of layers of bone tissue surrounding a central canal through which nerves and blood vessels run.

postmortem interval (PMI): The time between death and discovery of the corpse.

prognathism: Having jaws that project forward to a marked degree.

pupate: The transformation of an insect from larva to adult within a protective cocoon or hardened case.

rigor mortis: Stiffening of the body after death.

skeletonize: Reduce to a skeleton.

taphonomy: The study of a decaying organism over time.

For More Information

Books

Emily Craig, *Teasing Secrets from the Dead: My Investigations at America's Most Infamous Crime Scenes*. New York: Crown, 2004. Emily Craig writes of her experiences studying at the Body Farm and how it helped prepare her for her career as a forensic anthropologist.

N.E. Genge, *The Forensic Casebook*. New York: Ballantine, 2002. This book offers a relatively lively look at forensics.

David Owen, *Police Lab: How Forensic Science Tracks Down and Convicts Killers*. Buffalo, NY: Firefly, 2002. In this book, author David Owen discusses current methods of forensic investigation, highlighted by actual cases.

Periodicals

Diane Martindale, "Bodies of Evidence," *New Scientist*, January 6, 2001.

Emily Ramshaw, "Forensic Science: CSI-Style Unit Examines Bodies of Evidence—Neighbors May Object, but Research Helps Police Solve Cold Cases," *Dallas Morning News*, September 14, 2008.

Jessica Snyder Sachs, "The Fake Smell of Death," *Discover Magazine*, March 1996.

John A. Williams, "Study of Remains a Necessary Step in Solving Crimes," *Asheville Citizen-Times*, April 9, 2005.

Internet Sources

Shannon Lane, "Bodies May Rot in Campus 'Farm,'" *Orion Online*, May 16, 2007, http://media.www.theorion.com/media/storage/paper889/news/2007/05/16/Features/Bodies.May.Rot.In.Campus.farm-2897496.shtml.

Ted Rowlands, "Behind the Scenes: Body Hunt at Manson Ranch," *CNN.com*, May 9, 2008, www.cnn.com/2008/CRIME/05/08/bts.rowlands.manson/index.html#cnnSTCText.

Web Sites

American Board of Forensic Anthropology (www.theabfa.org). Provides information about ABFA board members and officers, the organization's policies and procedures, and information on forensic anthropology programs for students.

Bodies and Bones (http://whyfiles.org/192forensic_anthro/index.html). Provides articles and photographs detailing the practice of forensic anthropology. Also includes links to related files on forensic science, DNA fingerprinting, and other forensic topics.

University of Tennessee Forensic Anthropology Center (http://web.utk .edu/~anthrop/index.htm). Web site of the UT's Body Farm including its mission statement, details on collections and research projects, information on body donations, and answers to other frequently asked questions.

Index

Picture Credits

About the Author

Diane Yancey lives in the Pacific Northwest with her husband, Michael; their dog, Gelato; and their cats, Newton, Lily, and Alice. Yancey has written more than twenty-five books for middle-grade and high school readers, including *The Forensic Anthropologist, The Forensic Entomologist, The Case of the Green River Killer, The Unabomber,* and *The Zodiac Killer.*